In War
and Exile

*Thirty-eight
true stories*

Sally Hayton-Keeva

WSU
PRESS

Washington State University Press
Pullman, Washington

WASHINGTON STATE
UNIVERSITY

Washington State University Press
PO Box 645910
Pullman, Washington 99164-5910
Phone: 800-354-7360
Fax: 509-335-8568
E-mail: wsupress@wsu.edu
Web site: wsupress.wsu.edu

Originally published by City Lights Books, 1987.

Library of Congress Cataloging-in-Publication Data

Valiant women in war and exile.

   Bibliography: p.
   1. Valiant women in war and exile—Biography. 2. Military history, Modern—20th
century. I. Hayton-Keeva, Sally.

D412.5   920.72
ISBN 0-87422-263-X

YEARS   WSU PRESS
Fine Quality Books from the Pacific Northwest

For my husband, Joseph,
and my son, Blake

CONTENTS

Photo credits

By page number:

37. (top) Photograph © by Gary Wagner.
(bottom) Photograph by Janet Delaney.
38. (top) Courtesy of the California Committee for a Free Afghanistan.
(bottom) Photograph by Jeanne Hallacy.
39. (top) Photograph by Sara Colm.
40. (top) Photograph by Jeffrey Blankfort.
(bottom) Courtesy of the Jewish Community Library, San Francisco.
41. Photographs by John Giannini.
115. (bottom) Courtesy of Vietnam News Agency.
174., 177. (bottom) Courtesy of National Archives.
179. (top) Courtesy of National Archives.

INTRODUCTION TO WSU PRESS EDITION

Early one December morning in 1996, my father died of war injuries sustained half a century before. He had read *Valiant Women* when it was first published in 1987, and had never complained that I had told the truth about what war had done to him and, afterward, to his family.

I never knew the man my father might have been without World War II. I only knew him for the person he had become, the man who had peered into the caverns of hell and returned home, haunted and damaged, unable to forget what he had seen, unable to bear the stresses of fatherhood without anger, too burdened with guilt and grief and bitterness to simply be happy again. He never doubted the war needed to be fought, and I do not think he ever regretted volunteering in 1941 for a mission that would include Casablanca, Montecassino, and the landing on that bloody beach at Anzio.

His is a story repeated the world over by both men and women. As technology shortens the space between thought and action and removes the physical obstacles to female participation, women's war stories will become more familiar. Mythically, biologically, culturally, war may remain more of a male enterprise while female involvement may continue to be episodic and anomalous. We may always hear male voices raised the louder; but certainly, for better and for worse, we have entered an era in which women's war stories will no longer be uncommon.

There are women flying combat missions now, and there are women in the Pentagon. Women parachute into enemy territory. There has been a steady increase of women in the military since 1987, both in the United States and in armed forces around the world.

Nevertheless, the majority of women meet war as a stranger; one who disrupts or destroys the security of home. Unprepared by expectation, experience, or training, most women must deal with war the way they endure all challenges of life: abandonment and illness, sexual abuse and exile. These all are stories that need to be told.

Our time may be but an echo of time past, but there have been significant changes in the world since 1987. In that year I could write, "...we grew up in a country and town where we felt secure..." This may no longer be true for America's childen. The tentacles of global terrorism have overspread our increasingly interdependent world, making even small, rural towns unsafe. Throughout the world, children and women

suffer the horrors and indignities of war, and now we in America suffer them too. September 11 made it clear we can no longer consider ourselves removed from the front lines of war. All of us, at any time, may be called upon to be brave, to inspire others, to risk our lives, to serve. After *Valiant Women* was first published, I began speaking to groups about the roles women play in war. I was surprised to discover how emotional the subject was for many women, even those who had never experienced war firsthand. It was as if women had accepted the notion that battlefields have only male heroes and that women can only stand collectively in corners, waiting to be saved as they weep and wring their hands, victims who must look elsewhere for the courage to act and to survive.

When I was growing up, I used to dream I was a soldier, on a battlefield with other soldiers. The dream was always the same. Shot, I fell dying to the ground, my helmet rolling off and my long hair spilling out, disclosing the secret that I was female. The other soldiers crowded around me, amazed and admiring. "Look!" they cried to each other, "It's a woman!"

Women need only look inward for the strength to be warriors, to be war protestors, to be strong role models for their children. Given the right to speak, they can tell their stories and they can—at long last—come to terms with emotions they perhaps have long repressed. Myth and culture must broaden in scope so that the true nature of women and their life histories will be recorded and remembered, so that more of these previously unheard voices will echo in the distant future.

It has been profoundly moving over the past fifteen years to be told how the stories in this book have touched the hearts and lives of readers. That was what the women I interviewed devoutly wished. Ladan Jafari, who fled here with her family from Iran, is an actress and writer who adapted *Valiant Women* into a play. The first two performances in New York City in 2002 were fundraisers for women and girls in Afghanistan. Ladan wrote to me,

> I discovered *Valiant Women in War and Exile* when I was sixteen years old. It was an awkward time when I didn't know what my place was in the world. What was I capable of doing as a young woman? My parents said I could be anything I wanted to be, but was that true? There seemed

to be so many professions almost completely dominated by men: politicians, directors, writers, police officers, playwrights, engineers, doctors. My world of possibilities seemed small.

Valiant Women expanded this world exponentially with each story I read; the words of women who defied these small notions. I really could be *anything*. If girls younger than me could survive such atrocities and still continue on, then high school was not such a daunting task. I was deeply inspired and that inspiration has carried me through my life. Whenever I am faced with a "daunting task," I am reminded of these women and the obstacles that face me no longer seem so impossible.

I think about Ladan, with her life ahead of her. And I think about the women I interviewed whose lives have ended. Connie Dixon had become my best friend. I stood beside Tsengteh Wen's hospital bed as she lay dying and later wrote her obituary. I can still hear Marian Shelton's soft Southern voice. She was relentless in urging the government to find out the truth about her husband, missing in action in Vietnam. I heard on the radio the day she took her own life.

I have been honored to know all of these women and honored to be the vehicle to bring their stories to the world. Ladan wrote, "I now encourage women to defy the small notions and not be bogged down by them. To never be silent, for your words, experiences, and life are important."

Never let us be silent again.

INTRODUCTION TO CITY LIGHTS EDITION

This is a book about war. A book of war stories told not by men but by women—women who have fought in and suffered through and survived war.

We know the usual war stories; Hemingway wrote them, John Wayne acted them, Memorial Days put them into the news media. Bodies are counted, trenches dug, plasma transported, tactics discussed, bombs dropped, ships sunk. War seen through women's eyes makes a different kind of war story.

War speaks in a male voice to all of us. In my case it was my father, who has suffered lifelong war shock. He was a medic on the front lines in World War II for four years, and his sensitive nature was tortured by memories of this all the time my sister and I were growing up.

He would wake at night thinking he was under siege. In the early days he would duck every time a plane passed overhead, and in the little seaside town where I grew up in the fifties, he would sometimes carry me sleeping from my bed and leave me on the front lawn, evacuated from carnage. Sometimes he would wake us with his screaming, white with horror, reliving the three nights he spent in a ditch with twelve dead men. I remember him once sitting next to me in the living room with a book of photographs of men in his division, whispering in a broken voice, "This was Jim," or Bob or Gene, "He was killed at Anzio," or Montecassino or Rabat, while tears fell on the pages.

Mostly he told us exciting war stories. Escapades and near-misses. The story about his wandering the dark alleyways of a city in North Africa followed by a famous, scar-faced assassin. The time he and a buddy beat up some insulting Italians in a bar and, in their rapid departure before the M.P.'s arrived, his friend fell down a well. The purloined radio was another good one, and also the one about how Anzio Annie blew up the outhouse where my father had been moments before. This was my father's war when he was awake, and though he told us the kind of war stories we liked to hear, we could see in him the presence of a war he would

v

not discuss. He was the real war story for us. Easily angered, his rage was enormous, far greater than the childish misbehaviors that occasioned it. We were afraid of this side of him, and we tried never to make him angry, because when he wasn't angry he was whimsical and imaginative and kind. It was the soldier we feared.

This was our war, my sister's and mine, even though World War II was over before we were born. Even though we grew up in a country and a town where we felt secure, there was no one to protect us from the war inside our father. We didn't lock our doors in those safer times. There was no way we could keep war out.

In 1970 I was graduated from college and married a draft resister of the Vietnam War who had chosen to leave the U.S. rather than go to jail. We immigrated to Australia, which seemed like an adventure at the time although I also felt I was abandoning the antiwar movement so active then.

Soon after my son was born, I realized my marriage had been more politically than emotionally motivated, and that the political glue that once held us together had melted over time. I returned with my son to the U.S. in 1974. It seemed as if the war had been long over and already partly forgotten; as if those of us who had so passionately opposed it hardly existed anymore. Certainly women who had married resisters were not expected to have had any kind of valid "war story," just as so many women in the antiwar movement had been expected at political rap groups to keep quiet and make the coffee because it was men, and only men, who faced the draft.

On both sides of the front lines it was men who were making decisions and women who, more or less, passively accepted the decisions their men made. It was my husband who had the war story, such as it was. I did not—even though both of us had left to live in a foreign country 8,000 miles from home.

Mine isn't much of a war story, but my experiences were the catalyst for this book. I knew at a very early age that the effects of war know no boundaries and that wars never end. Later I learned that women who experience the effects of war, if not war itself, are expected to be silent.

In my mind's eye there is an enormous kaleidoscope, and in every fragment of colored glass there is a woman's face, and every

face belongs to a woman who lives with the effects of war. That kaleidoscope is the world today. I could find women's war stories in every village and town and city in every country on earth, and not two of those stories would be the same. The accounts in this book are only a sampling. They cover the entire 20th century. Beginning with the most contemporary wars, a woman guerrilla fighter tells of her life in the mountains outside San Salvador. There follow first-person stories of the invasion of Afghanistan, conflicts in Southeast Asia, Northern Ireland and the Middle East. Women recall their experiences in Vietnam, World War II, the Spanish civil war, back through China's revolutions and the 1915 Turkish massacre of Armenians.

As if the book suddenly had a life of its own the moment I conceived it, I began to meet women with fascinating war stories. Yet, there were unexpected difficulties. I placed ads in newspapers and magazines, but very few were answered; and no one from a U.S. governmental body or military installation ever replied to a letter or returned my many phone calls. Most of the women I finally interviewed were located through networks of mutual acquaintances and organizations.

There were days I stood on streetcorners, waiting for a car to pick me up and take me to a secret location. There were rooms in old buildings where I was carefully scrutinized before being allowed to enter and the door locked behind me. There were cups of coffee in suburban living rooms. There were people who never showed up for the interview and those who had to postpone them time and time again because of fear or anxiety.

I was, and am, deeply touched and grateful for the trust these women had in me and for the courage it took for many of them to speak of their pain, their bravery, their secrets—face to face with a stranger. Without portfolio, with the backing only of my husband, I began. With new understanding, and with the trust and emotional generosity of all the 55 women I interviewed, this book is done.

I admit that my initial concept of woman as innocent victim and pacifist was more comfortable than the panoply of motives and skills and qualities I found. These first-person narratives chal-

lenge the popular idea of war as an act of protection, in that women's lives are generally every bit as threatened in a combat zone; and they counter the stereotype of women as a madonna to be protected from the plundering enemy (whose women are generally stereotyped as whores and therefore available for the rape and abuse common in war). They also challenge the notion that if women had a voice in the conduct of war and in the formulation of war policy, they would automatically oppose violence. Given a practical reason, women fight hard and effectively. Behind the scenes, they have supported their fighting men, and their attitudes can encourage war. This does not mean to say, however, that women cannot also be courageous and passionate pacifists, but these voices are more traditionally heard.

Listening to the women in this book speak, I realized I was hearing stories that were not about heroism and power and glory, but about the "little things" that have less to do with war than with the human condition. Men, who often have no other outlet for the experience of intimate relationship or emotional display, perhaps remember their war years with a conscious or unconscious nostalgia for them. Life, perhaps, will never again give them such moments of camaraderie and shared emotion. Their war stories are a reenactment of ceremony, a dedication to sentiment. Women, on the other hand, tell war stories that are not separated from the rest of their physical and emotional lives; war is part of the fabric of living. Before the war, life was. After war, life for the survivors remains to be lived. There are children to care for and meals to cook and friends to confide in. War is not suspended in time, something outside a woman's experience of life; it is part of life, woven into all the rest.

Ever since 60 A.D.—and probably long before that—when Queen Boadicea challenged the Roman Empire to battle, there have been women warriors. They have been cloaked in myth and mystery and their historical importance often trivialized, but their stories remain tantalizing reminders that it isn't only a man who can become a hero in combat.

However, because of cultural restrictions, women who become warriors are few. As John Stuart Mill observed in 1869, "Women are what we have required them to be." Still, the legacy of the

woman warrior exists, on every continent. For example, there is Hind-al-Hunud, who encouraged her Arabian clan to fight against the domination of Mecca by Mohammed, and who argued for her husband's death after he surrendered the city. Women in Afghanistan today vividly recall her fierce resolve.

In the West Joan of Arc became a legend. The conscience of Charles VI, burned at the stake for "heresy," she was in fact put to death for her tenacity in resisting English encroachments upon her native France.

In our American revolution of 1775, and the subsequent wars on our soil, women have been involved in combat, most often through subterfuge. It has been estimated that in the Civil War over four hundred women served in the Union Army, disguised as men.

Spanish women fought valiantly in the militias against fascist forces in the civil war, and women from around the world joined them in the International Brigades. Women were trained in the use of weapons in World War I. In World War II, women entered the armed forces particularly where male forces were insufficient. Female volunteers were pilots and snipers and spies, while other women were active in the resistance to Nazi invasion and persecution.

Women have been drafted into Israel's armed forces since 1949. Although few have fought on the front, some have asked to serve there. All receive battle training, however, and are instructed in the use of firearms. Today women fight in the Palestinian army and as guerrillas in Central America. In Nicaragua, the Sandinista Army utilized hundreds of women, many of whom rose in the ranks to leadership positions in the military. In Afghanistan in the 1980s, women have taken up weapons that dwindling male forces have left behind.

Women like these who have volunteered in wars are especially courageous because they were not conscripted to risk their lives. They did so by choice. Such women are to be found all over the world, fighting for their countries, for their families, for their beliefs, for themselves.

One Vietnam veteran officer—later a C.I.A. operative—spoke to me about the female volunteers he took with his men to help flush

out nests of the Viet Cong along the coastal plains.

"Most of these women had volunteered for the best reason in the world—they had a score to settle. These were women who had lost their entire families in the Tet Offensive, had seen them lined up against walls and shot. These women were embued with a deep and almost boiling hatred, hatred at the very soul, the kind of hatred that if it were directed at me I'd want to move to another planet.

"As for women in combat, I would have absolutely no reservations at any time of taking them into combat with me—if they had been told the truth and had a reason to be there. Flagwaving may be enough to motivate men, but women need to know why a war is necessary and what would happen if it weren't fought. Pragmatic things, not flagwaving, apple pie or glory."

Then, there are the vast numbers of women, not actively involved in combat themselves, who have supported their troops in myriad official and unofficial capacities. Women have eased the privations and terrors of war in many ways—as nuns working selflessly where bloody revolutions are being waged; or as prostitutes who open their arms to men that war has scarred. There are flight attendants serving boys on the way to and from the battlefields; and nurses who fight to save lives and who, more than anyone else in wartime, see war in all its horror. In fact, it was women's historical employment as nurses—most often without pay or recognition—that actually led to the opening of the U.S. Military to thousands of female volunteers in World War II. Even in World War I, more than 100,000 women had worked in munitions factories and in other jobs traditionally held by men.

In 1942, the U.S. Navy's WAVES (Women Accepted for Volunteer Emergency Services) was created. WAVE Commander Elizabeth Reynard commented dryly, "I figure the word 'Emergency' will comfort the older admirals, because it implies that we're only a temporary crisis and won't be around for keeps." WAVES held down 75% of the jobs at Radio Washington, the heart of Naval Communications at the time, and more than 105,000 WAVES handled the fleet's mail service.

In the United States by World War II, there were over 180,000 women in active service in various auxiliary branches of the mil-

itary. Additionally, three million American women joined women from other countries in the International Red Cross.

In spite of this massive contribution, it wasn't until 1948 that women were given permanent status in the U.S. armed forces through the passage of the Women's Armed Services Act. This tardy recognition of what women can and do contribute is not unusual. While working on this book, I was variously told that somewhere between 5,000 and 50,000 women served in Vietnam. Give or take 45,000, it doesn't seem to matter.

Women both inside and outside the U.S., of course, have not always waited for government policy to give them employment in war. They've become spies and couriers, medics and revolutionaries and Rosie the Riveters because they felt they had a patriotic duty to do so, because survival required it, or simply because they needed a job.

Then there are the mothers, the widows, the exiles. Women give birth to sons and daughters whom, after all their care and love, they must lose to war. They must bury loved ones and leave the graves behind. They must hide children and feed children and carry them when they're too weak from hunger to walk. They must care for the permanently disabled. They must endure rape and abuse of both body and spirit and manage to go on.

If they have survived, they take up their lives again. The vast majority of women in war simply disappear, back to where they came from or to somewhere new and alien. If they have fled persecution in their own country, or have been driven as refugees from it, they must learn to survive as "foreigners" in distant, perhaps unwelcoming, lands. Those who do remain at home, but with their lives utterly changed, go back to work in the house or outside of it, pay taxes, bake cakes, raise children, wash socks, compose music, invite friends over, mend the fence.

There are Cambodian refugees down the street and Holocaust survivors upstairs and the corner grocery is run by a Palestinian woman who feels bitterly homeless. War, seen from the heart and liberated from jargon and statistics, becomes like a stone thrown into a pond, altering its surface with concentric circles that leave nothing untouched.

The women in this book are not necessarily stronger or wiser

than most women. Each one would deny being so. Some are uni-
que because they have survived the most horrendous catastrophes
of the past century. Even these remarkable women did not seem so
uncommon to me when I spoke with them; they were as common
or uncommon as women generally are. What these valiant women
do, however, is hold up mirrors in which most women, like and
unlike them, can glimpse their own reflections and recognize
qualities and concerns they share.

Not all of these stories are sensational. Some women had
quieter experiences and told, nonetheless, stories both perceptive
and interesting. I included women who were in war the way men
often are; behind the scenes as secretaries and chauffeurs, away
from the action, pushing pencils.

As I tracked women down through political, religious and
social groups, through friends and strangers, my awareness grew
that war is not a foreign, distant event, neatly packaged by begin-
nings and endings, pertaining to one point in time. It is far too
convenient to bracket wars in dates. Peace treaties may record the
end of a war and attempt to guarantee war will not happen again,
but they're only meaningless pieces of paper. For, in fact, we live
in a world of continual war: 300 of them, at least, since the end of
World War II.

I started this book thinking I would meet passive victims, but I
didn't. I thought I would hear much the same sad story from the
women I interviewed, but I was wrong. I thought I'd hear a lot of
blame laid at the male door, but that rarely happened. We are just
beginning to find out what women have done, what women are
capable of being and doing and thinking, and without that
knowledge we are missing a crucial link in understanding not
only the process of warfare, but the human condition, itself.

War is timeless, and it may be something that is rooted in us, in
what it is to be a human being. If that is so, and if we are to
survive, it is important to investigate the parts played by women
in war, it's time to listen to what they have to say. Women have
been encouraged culturally to keep silent, unless they are telling
stories pacifistic in nature or intent. It is clear that we need to
know much more about gender and war, and about why women
have been excluded from war's discourse.

In the following stories, we hear how women took active command of their lives when they needed to do so. Whether they were fighting at the front, working in an army hospital or in the underground, confined in a concentration camp or adjusting to exile, all of them now speak of how they dealt with grief and terror and loss and did what had to be done. Acting with intelligence and passion, with courage, and often with grace, they taught me that love and spirit and strength are what women are—in war, and also, in peace.

Sally Hayton-Keeva

KARLA RAMIREZ

Karla Ramirez, a guerrilla who lives in the mountains near San Salvador, fights to end the desperate poverty in her country by overthrowing the government.

EL SALVADOR

I grew up in the capital of San Salvador. My family was not poor and so it was not until high school that I met all different kinds of people, many very poor girls and boys. The house I had grown up in was not very big, but we had everything we needed. Suddenly I was going to the houses of my friends, and I thought it was impossible for anyone to live the way they did.

I remember one friend I had whose mother made tortillas for a living. I saw her little brothers playing in the dirt, with no clothes on, eating whatever they found on the ground. I saw many people like that around me, and then when I went to the country to do social work, I saw what life was like for the farmers. It was a life of poverty and hardship. That's why I started fighting. It wasn't for myself but for my people and what was happening to them.

When I went to the University, I studied anaesthesiology, which I liked. I thought I could someday work in a hospital and help the poor; but, when I was eighteen years old, I learned what it was I had to do instead. At first I wasn't in the B.P.R. (Popular Revolutionary Bloc), but I worked with them. There was a lot of repression of young people and students in the capital because they knew we had the heart to fight. After awhile I met more people in the group, and they found in me the feelings they were looking for, and so I was allowed to join. We used to go to B.P.R. meetings in the morning, to the University in the afternoon, and we studied at night.

Our group is clandestine. The military doesn't know who is in it, so they kill some people who are members, and they also kill

some who aren't members just because they suspect them of belonging. The first thing the government forces do if they capture anyone in the B.P.R. is torture them to get information. What you have to do is to endure it and keep your mouth shut. You already know what you are supposed to say and what you cannot. And then they kill you.

I think about being captured sometimes, but I'm not afraid. When I think about it, I pray, "Please God, don't let me talk. If they torture me, please give me the strength to keep quiet." Many of our people have died because of someone talking. I have many people behind me, around me, and they can't die because of me.

I always did whatever my leader told me to do. In the beginning, we would go out on the streets at night and put posters on the lamp posts. We knew the government forces suspected us and were following us. You are taught to recognize when the police or the military are following you, and after awhile you feel their presence on the street or in a store. You learn to be like an animal with an animal's nose and ears.

I had a girlfriend who was in the B.P.R. with me. One night we were studying together for a test we had at the University the next day. When I went to take the test the next morning she wasn't there. I was too upset to take the test. I went to my compañeros and we started looking for her, but we couldn't find her. Three days later they found her body lying on the ground beside a street.

I drove with some friends to where the body was. There were many people standing around it, but I could see right away that it was my friend. I can't explain to you how I felt. What do you feel when you look at your best friend and her head has been cut off? She was almost seven months pregnant, and they had cut open her stomach and put her dead baby between her legs, and then they had put her head inside her stomach where the baby had been. We had felt that her baby would be another son of the revolution; now he was dead, too.

All I could think of was who could do something like that? I wanted a gun at that moment and I wanted to go to the police and kill every single one of them. The military does things like that every day. They don't just kill one person a day, they kill hundreds. Thousands and thousands of people have been killed, and not just quickly with a bullet. They rape women, they tor-

ture, they do everything you can imagine. They come out of nowhere and knock on your door at night and take people away in trucks. You have to watch them take away your family, and often you don't know why because they haven't even done anything the government thinks is wrong.

Many people are missing and their families don't know if they're dead or alive or in jail. There's a mothers' committee of women whose children have disappeared, and they have the faith to keep searching for them. They ask the military, "Please, just tell us if they are still alive." But the government doesn't care for their feelings. Thousands and thousands of people have died like that, taken away and killed and buried somewhere, and their family will never know what happened or where they are buried.

One night the military took away my cousin, who was eighteen. We never knew why. Sometimes they take pictures of the corpses, however, and so that is how I know what they did to him: they burned him to death with torches. That was another reason I had to fight.

In 1980, I realized I had to go to the mountains and help the compañeros to fight and to help with the wounded. At first I was scared to go because I thought about what could happen to me and also because I had a baby son just four months old. I didn't know anything about living like the compañeros, but when they told me what it was for, what I could contribute there, I no longer thought only about myself. It was hard to get away from all the things I was used to having, but you have to separate from all that. Now I don't miss those things at all.

Members of the organization came to my house at about five o'clock, when it was still dark. I took my *mochila*, my backpack, and went with them. My husband understood why I had to go. He was in the organization, too, but he had to stay in San Salvador. My mother was very upset about my leaving because she knew it was dangerous work, but she was also upset because I left my baby with her. She was forty-six years old and also in the organization, along with my father, and it was going to be hard for her to go to the meetings now that she had to take my baby along. It was very, very hard to leave him. I cried. But I knew what I did was for my baby, and not only for him, but for everybody, because for me everybody is my son.

3

I had been breast-feeding him, so I had to take a breast pump with me into the mountains to take the milk out. In Latin America the people are very modest, but I had to learn not to care about doing that in front of my compañeros. It is really so beautiful to live in common with the people. Some women gave birth in the mountains and didn't have much milk, so I gave my milk to them for their babies. We didn't have enough food there, and babies get so hungry.

Sometimes I would think, "Is this truly what I have to do? To leave my baby and come here?" Sometimes, in the beginning, I got confused.

Early on you learn all about the struggle and you meet your compañeros, but you don't learn any names. He is just your compañero, and she is just your compañera. That's the only way you know them, because if the military would take you away later, and they did things like pull off your fingernails and cut your fingers off or put nails through your hands, how do you know whether or not you could keep quiet?

In the mountains I learned how to crawl so the enemy couldn't see me coming close, and I learned to roll along the ground to avoid the bullets. I learned to climb, to protect myself, and to hide from the enemy. I learned to use all kinds of weapons, including the M-19. It was hard to carry and hard to learn how to open it and clean it and then assemble it again very fast. You had to know exactly how many seconds it took to clean your weapon because sometimes you don't know if the enemy is nearby or not and you have to be prepared always.

It's beautiful being there. The feeling in the camp is often happy. You can listen to the music of your people, you can pick fruit or make tortillas with your compañeros and sit together and eat. Usually the cooking is done by women from the countryside, poor people who come to live with us. They usually do the things we don't have time to do, like cooking and washing. They do it, not because they are our maids, but because they know they are our compañeros.

The first mission I had was to stop a convoy of weapons along the highway. Every time there is a convoy we have to stop it because most of our weapons come from the military.

There were twenty-five of us on my first mission. We went

down the mountain on foot in the amount of time we had been told to take. You know the soldiers will start shooting right away and you have to be prepared for that.

When I saw that first convoy coming, I felt the hair on my skin stand up, I was so scared. But when they came close enough for me to see them, then I didn't feel any fear. When the soldiers saw us they wanted to run away, but we had them surrounded and they had to fight.

I have fought many times, but that first time was not easy. I had to keep in mind that these are people who had killed someone in my family, and as long as I kept thinking that, I knew I could kill them. While I was waiting, I thought, "I cannot, cannot." Then, when the convoy came, I knew I could. There is no choice but to kill, you have to demonstrate to your compañeros that you can. You know everybody is scared. If you ran away, others might do the same and it would be your fault.

It is hard to kill someone. I have to keep my compañeros in mind, a special, very human feeling, and then I can do it. I have cried sometimes for what I have had to do. Compañeros will say, "Don't. You do not need to demonstrate to your compañeros what you are feeling." But sometimes you can't stand it. You are human. Men would cry too, sometimes, but no one would say anything to them about what they were feeling because they would be embarrassed. When I cry all those things that make me feel bad seem farther away, and I feel much better. I pray, "God, what can I do? I have to do this because there is no other way to make people understand that this struggle has to be." I make myself strong by thinking about my cousin and my girlfriend, but most of all I think about my son. I think about all the people who are waiting for the liberation of our country, and that every time I fight I help to win that struggle.

Sometimes we take prisoners, but we do not kill anyone after we have taken control of the weapons. We do not feel that they have to die just to die. Often they are boys just sixteen or seventeen years old, and we feel like they could be our brother or our compañero and that sometime later they might join us. Many of them do.

I stayed in the mountains for five months the first time and went on twenty missions. We didn't only fight, but went into the

5

towns and took control of them so we could speak to the people, to give them the conscience to help us. We know there are people who don't understand us. They are not educated and have been told lies. However, many people leave the towns with us and go to the mountains. It's hard to take care of the children, especially since we have to move from place to place, but we can't leave them behind. They want to be with us; they don't want to go home, even the very little children. Even five-year-olds want to learn how to fight with guns, but we don't train them until they are ten. We have to be aware when they're ready for certain things.

In our group there are about two hundred and fifty women and almost seven hundred men. There is really no difference between us. A woman can become a leader the same as a man and do everything a man can do.

We all hold the same desire in our hearts. We only want to have justice, and liberty. We want to have our own houses and enough money to live on. Fourteen families in my country have everything, and there are people who are dying because they don't have enough food or medicine. How can you feel nothing when a child is dying because he can't get a shot to cure his tuberculosis? When you plant a seed and care for it, why when it grows up can't you keep it to feed your child?

I think the feeling I have is the same feeling that many women have, and if they have my feeling then they should go ahead and not be afraid to die to change things. If you die you leave behind your heart to the people who follow, to your child who comes after you.

ELLEN NEARY

Ellen Neary, a Roman Catholic nun who assisted Indians and refugees on the Mexico-Guatemala border, reassessed the responsibilities of her faith in response to conditions in Central America.

MEXICO • GUATEMALA

I entered the religious life in 1955, right after I finished high school. I had read a lot of books about people who helped other people, books about Dorothy Day and Mother Cabrini and Tom Dooley, and those people seemed to be leading lives that made sense to me.

I taught school for eight years, and then in 1963 my life changed. There was a feeling of more missionary spirit in the United States, especially since the Pope had asked religious orders in North America to share both personal and financial resources with the Church in Latin America.

Our Mother General was given the task of setting up a mission in the little town of Ocosingo in the jungles of Chiapas, Mexico, very near the border of Guatemala. The area was being newly inhabited by Indians who were getting land through the Mexican Reform Laws.

But in 1972, it was evident that there was no more land to give away. Some of the land already settled proved to have possible oil reserves and stands of valuable hardwood trees, and President Echeverria had it declared an "ecological reserve." Two large unrelated Indian tribes made a much larger group of people than they were used to, and the result was fatal to them. Among strangers, they couldn't choose leadership and began to distrust each other. The whole cultural structure began to fall apart.

Government agencies came in and took control of the leadership, and the tribes dissolved. People suffered from this tremendously.

7

What happened to the Chol people was sadder still. They were moved right down on the Guatemalan border where there was very little population. I guess the Mexican government, in 1975, saw the civil problems in Guatemala coming to a head, and these Indians were moved down to "Frontier Echeverria," across the river from Guatemala. The people were given tarred roofing to build very rudimentary housing before they went out to clear the jungle and plant their crops in order to survive. They were promised corn and beans until their crops could be harvested. The food was flown in for a while, but there was never enough of it and the people were forced to eat roots and berries or whatever they could find.

In 1981, when the Guatemalan Army swept across the northern border and annihilated some Indian and Spanish-speaking communities in that area, the people from Luz de Alma fled across the river to seek refuge with the Mexicans they had become friendly with. The Chol people were more than happy to give them refuge because they were very aware that the Guatemalans had helped them in their hour of need. In fact, they were so willing to help that they offered to go across the river and help fight off the Guatemalan Army. More astute members of the community said it was a bigger problem than they could handle and sent a delegation to the state capital to advise the governor that they had refugees with them and that the Guatemalan Army was right across the river. We went down to see what we could do to help the refugees, but the Mexican army had gotten there ahead of us and asked us to wait until the Guatemalans were more settled before we saw them.

As we went on up the Usomacinta River to visit some other new Mexican communities that were being formed along the riverside, we heard more and more tragic and horrifying stories about what had been happening to the Guatemalans. The new Mexican settlers had seen many bodies that had been tied together and then thrown into the river. A lot of these new settlers had no idea what a political boundary was and they didn't know if what was happening in Guatemala was going to happen next to them. They were utterly terrified and would probably have moved out of the area had they been able to. But the launches are controlled by the Mexican government agencies and there were no roads, so they

had to stay here during this massacre, watching the bodies of victims floating on the river.

The feeling I experienced most of all was admiration for the tremendous ability of these people to sustain suffering. They had been abruptly moved into the jungle area; they were suffering from malaria and typhoid fever; the children were suffering from dysentery. Many died. It was difficult to explain to the villagers what was happening and who was doing the killing and that the river was a natural border between the two countries and that the Guatemalan soldiers were not supposed to cross the river, which they did at a later time, however.

When we came back down the river and found out that the refugees had all been sent back to Guatemala by the Mexican Army, I felt betrayed that I had been fooled. We had trusted them. Now this happened because the army had no way to feed the refugees and did not want contact between the Mexican and Guatemalan populations because it was afraid that guerrillas were in with the refugees and didn't want the Mexican people to be politicized by them.

The refugees I worked with later were composed of women who were widows and children who were orphans. The men had been killed by the Guatemalan Army, which had been raiding the villages and killing civilians at random. Their stories were very gruesome, about people being picked off because of vengeance, or arbitrarily because they might be guerrillas. Some men wouldn't join either side, the guerrillas or the army, and they were looked at as potential guerrilla members and shot.

It's beyond belief how people can be so brutalized. Indian people are very peaceful by nature. Their life is hard, and then to put on top of that such violence—it's like the straw that broke the camel's back. I think that is why so many of them have joined the guerrillas. They've suffered enough from a system that ignores them, and then to have that system commit genocide is just too much to bear.

When the refugees came back the second time, their numbers had lessened, and we realized their families were being decimated. There was the terrible worry about who would take care of whole villages of widows and orphans. I guess when a religious person experiences something like this, you begin to question God. If He

9

is almighty and He loves us, why doesn't He help these poor people?

I think that's where the greatest experience of all came for us, because we, the outsiders, the religious community, began to be frustrated and question God, but the Indian people didn't. When they gather around and talk about their experiences, what they say is, "This is something we have to suffer for our country to be free." Bitterness doesn't seem to be there at all. They believe they have a right to their land which is something I think the Church has encouraged them over the last few years to believe.

When we sisters reflected together about what we were doing down there, we said, "It seems they have a faith that makes them submissive to a way of life that could change." We began to think about how their faith could become instrumental in helping them better their own situation, how their faith could make them active instead of passive. I think they related a lot to God as the Father, the Creator, and themselves as his submissive children. But they were not very well-acquainted with Jesus Christ. So through reflections with them we tried to get them to know Jesus as a man among men who was open to God working in Him, who was sensitive to the plight of the poor in his own country and tried to make their lives more dignified.

The Catechists realized that this interpretation of Christ's teaching puts them on the line in a militant way, and some of them would rather be passive because it's safer. Once you believe God is on your side, you're on a side. Christianity has been guilty of preaching more about the hereafter than the here-and-now, as if life is too hard to deal with. It's easier to deal with a life hereafter which you know very little about, and if you can get people interested in that, then you don't have to deal with their everyday problems. That's very convenient.

It really didn't seem so radical a teaching at the time, but now I can see that it is because what it suggests is a profound structural change. The old belief puts people in a certain social structure and keeps them there. So when the Indians started to realize they had a right to land—something that had begun with the Land Reform Laws in the Constitution of Mexico, but had not gone far enough because of other social structures that served to keep the Indians still in "their place"—they started to become militant, and

this is not only in the case of Mexico, but in other countries in Latin America where the people are beginning to rise against oppression.

I did journey into Guatemala with another sister during the Christmas of 1981. There were large numbers of Indian people being moved by soldiers and many trucks passed us full of soldiers with their rifles pointed toward the mountains as if they were expecting the guerrillas to begin firing at them. The country had the distinct atmosphere of being under occupation. Soldiers were everywhere and in control, and there was a feeling that anybody who wasn't a soldier was somehow an enemy of the army. To see the Indians being hurried away somewhere, and to wonder, "How will these families survive?" was so saddening. We were told later that they were being moved to strategic villages; and, since the food there is controlled by the army, the Indians would be forced to do as the army said.

After we visited the Catechists and it was time to leave, we all shook hands and they said, "We'll see one another tomorrow if God wants." It was a common way of taking one's leave, but it was very meaningful in that situation, since it was so likely some of them might not be around for the next meeting. Some of them might have to disappear, others would be shot.

We went to visit Sister Tony, who is very independent. I'd worked with her before and had always been impressed by her strength. But when I went up to greet her, she grabbed hold of my hand in a way she had never held it before. She needed someone right then, she was at the point of absolute desperation.

That night I sat with the sisters and they were so much in need of talking out their experiences, of talking about their confrontations with soldiers and about the atrocities they'd seen, about the amount of fear that had built up in them. One of the girl's brothers had been killed before the eyes of her family. Their activities were very limited and they seemed to be suffering a kind of siege mentality.

I went back toward the border to visit some other sisters who were friends of mine. It was New Year's Eve when I arrived and they were going to have a prayer service. It was an unforgettable experience for me, sitting with these women as each in turn thanked God very calmly for His blessings in the old year and

11

asking for His peace in the new year. By the time it came to my turn to pray I was in tears. That these people living in such an oppressive situation could thank God for a year that had brought such horror to the people they lived with! To ask for peace and to ask for it so tranquilly overwhelmed me. I was the only one in the room who was crying. I said to them, "I can't understand! You have seen so much horror in this country and yet you stay so calm!" They replied, "We've had to learn this attitude from the people. It's how they've managed to deal with their situation and survive. That's something they've taught us."

I returned to Chiapas. Our regional team of missionaries then established a solidarity group with the refugees and worked with them full time, since by June of 1982 we had a few thousand Guatemalans in our area, which has risen to 12,000 now and 40,000 in the diocese. There are many more thousands elsewhere. They are being allowed to stay in Mexico now, and the Church has been given more latitude in dealing with them. There has been a drought in Chiapas and corn and beans are now in short supply, so donated food is all they have to depend on. Food is severely rationed in the camps, which has been a tremendous worry to us. Many children are coming over from Guatemala terribly undernourished, several hundred have had to be treated in our mission hospital. Some of the people have been told that if they take food from the missionaries then they can't have any from the government agency, which is not a policy, just local mishandling.

Since there are so many widows with children to support, our mission has set up cooperatives for making and marketing the beautiful weaving Guatemalan women do. The sisters are the mobile people because the refugees aren't allowed to leave their camps, and we bring in the materials and then take out the finished work and try to find markets for it. The women do a little farming if someone allows it, and the children are getting some kind of schooling. It's important for all of them to have something to do.

It has become a life very different from the one I first envisioned. When I first entered the convent we had a very monastic spirituality, praying the Office, the official prayers of the Church, at certain hours. When, in Chiapas, we moved away from the monastic form of prayer, which was inappropriate to a ministry

12

that kept very odd hours in constantly changing places, a new spirituality had to develop that would be appropriate. In Chiapas we have been faced with life and death issues, with terrible inequities. We had to learn to deal with them in prayer. Sharing our reflections became a kind of prayer.

When I went down to Mexico I thought I had something to give the people, a message of faith. I was really surprised when I found out that these people have more faith in God than I had, or will ever have. So the work was different from what I had ever envisioned. It wasn't engendering faith or even nurturing faith; it had to do with my own perspective of faith changing. And that was a group process. We realized that faith has to inform and change and transform life, and make it a dignified vehicle of human existence. I think the only alternative we have to that is annihilation.

What the Catholic Church has actually been doing has been educating Central American people, the poor people, and I think a lot of the revolution that has been taking place down there is because of that education. If the result of education is revolution, then I think it's a very legitimate result of that education. Although violence in any form repels me, nonviolence in response to oppression hasn't worked. What does the entire Church do to accept the responsibility of the educating it has done? You don't just educate people in a vacuum. Education is revolutionary. When people come to a different point than where they were before being educated, you're responsible for getting them there.

I've had to look at my own lifestyle and my way of dealing with people, even my own citizenship. I have to be responsible for my own country, and I can't deny that I'm an American, as much as I deplore U.S. policies in Central America. What is more, I have to be responsible for my own faith. It's easy to blame God. The whole idea of the Incarnation is that God works through us, but here we are expecting Him to work outside of us, to perform some miracles that will mesmerize us all and get us back into line again.

That's not the way God works. Man is God's great risk. He gave us free will, and we have that free will to either make the world a better place or let it blow itself up. We are the ones who have to take the challenge, and bring peace back on earth.

13

Nazifa Afghan, a teacher with anticolonialist convictions, resisted Soviet invaders of her country, then fled through the Kyber Pass during guerrilla fighting in 1981.

AFGHANISTAN

I am from a Pashtoon family. The Pashtoon people are stricter Muslims than the people who speak Farsi. We are instructed by our families not to work in a job after marrying, but I had a strong feeling that I must be useful to Afghanistan. I was college-educated and felt there was much I could do to help my country. So I really had two problems in the 1970s: one inside the home with my disapproving family; and one outside with the Communists. I was fortunate that my husband is a sensible man. He studied medicine in West Germany, and he gave me the necessary permission to work outside my home teaching at a high school in Kabul.

The coup against our government by the Communist Party was the beginning of the drama. I was a witness when they seized power. First, they threw away our religious books from the mosques. The Communists would say, "Don't waste your time reading the Koran because it isn't useful for your future. It's not a science. First you have to start with science."

They changed the curriculum and brought in a new subject, "politics." So we had a demonstration against teaching it. Then the government sent troops of soldiers to separate the teachers from the students. The girls were throwing stones at the soldiers and breaking off the legs from chairs to attack them. We teachers encouraged our students to do this. The whole school demonstrated many, many times. Once, all of the students were inside the classroom with me and we broke up the chairs and threw them out of the third floor windows in protests against the Com-

14

munists, and soldiers came to our classroom and hit the students and pulled out handfuls of their hair. I fell down on the floor with them and we covered our heads, but they shocked us with electric rods and kicked us in the head.

We started rebelling in the schools because we felt the government wouldn't make as much trouble in the classrooms as they would with regular people outside. I had my students study revolutionary poems, but soon the administration said, "You may not use these poems any longer in your teaching." But I felt I had to teach them. Especially the poems of Malalai, a very great poet who wrote during the time the Afghans fought the English. When I read what she had written about the revolution, the students cried. I was glad to see this—I wanted to move them, to shake up their feelings. Every revolution starts with educated people. We wanted to start a revolution against the Communist government.

After our students began demonstrating against the Russian troops that had invaded Afghanistan in 1981, the Russians made strict rules. Students and teachers were not allowed off campus. One day, there was a very big demonstration and I wanted to join the students. After I had gone home to breastfeed my two small children, I requested permission to go, but the administration wouldn't let me. Later that evening we were told that one of my students, Nahid, and her two girlfriends had been killed in the street by machine guns. That is one of the worst memories of my life because I loved her very much. I was proud of the way she died. She stood there saying, "Allah-o-Akbar" over and over, even while they shot her down. They had to shoot her five times before she fell dead.

After a short time the Soviets started doing other dangerous things. They mixed chemicals in the water at school and the students got sick. The Communists tried to lay the blame on the freedom-fighters because they wanted us to think badly of the Mujahedin. They had help in this from the students who were in the Communist Party. The Soviets also took many girls who demonstrated to the Pul-i-Charkhy, a famous, very large jail where people are tortured.

In our culture it is forbidden for unmarried girls to have sexual relations, but I saw many girls come out of that jail pregnant. Many of them had been raped as well as tortured. If a woman who

15

had a fiance was raped, then the fiance and his family had to kill her. Many women and girls have been raped by Russian soldiers. The people are powerless to stop them because they can only fight with words, the Russians have the guns.

In the cases of most of the women who are raped, we only saw their bodies afterward. Whether they were killed by the rape or by the Russians or by themselves, we don't know. You see, it is shameful in Islam for women to be raped and continue to live in such disgrace. If I had been in that position, I would have found some medicine that would have killed me, or I would have escaped the city to the top of the mountains and jumped, or gone down to the river and drowned. I would never have gone back to my husband. I could never have gone back to his home with a bad name. I would not mind dying if that happened to me because maybe some people would hear of it and feel bad for me and my family and take revenge on the Russians. My death would be very worthwhile then.

A few of my students were agents of the Russians and were there as spies in my class, so the Communists always knew I was teaching revolution against them. They warned me that if I continued, I would be taken to Pul-i-Charkhy jail. Often I felt afraid when I was going to and from school because of the constant fire of machine guns in the streets. Finally, I stopped teaching and stayed home. I really wanted to be a freedom-fighter by then, but there weren't any weapons for me. I also worried about my children— who would support and take care of them?

Three times Communists searched my home. I had some jewelry and some books and they took everything. When they came to the door, I held up the Koran in front of me and said, "Don't destroy us. Just search our home and leave us alone. We have no weapons." They took the Koran and threw it to the ground. Russians do not think at all about our customs and culture. They aren't human; they're like animals!

It was hard to talk with friends about what was happening because we weren't allowed to be in groups or to contact each other, so during prayers in the mosques we whispered about what was going on. Maybe there were spies in the mosques, because soon the Russians started bombing the mosques, too.

My aunt was living in Herat, and they bombed her home and

killed her children, and so she came to live with us in Kabul. She told us how one day there was a demonstration against the Communist government. No, a revolution! Men and women, some with weapons and some with only stones, attacked the government's soldiers, and 24,000 people were killed. Russian and Afghan troops were fighting the people, one to one, with guns and knives and stones. There was no difference in the men and women who fought. Shoulder to shoulder they fought against the enemy, with no difference between them, as we saw for ourselves in the Packtia Province when we were escaping through it to Pakistan. In this area many men have become freedom-fighters, and half of the men have been killed, so their women have had to stand guard and warn the Mujahedin of the presence of the enemy. They were armed and fought the Russians, too, old women and young women, both. Every night I spent thinking about fighting the Russians. I knew I was as strong as a man, an Afghani man, but my position for fighting was very bad because I had two small children and no gun. Otherwise, I would have been ready. This is what I still dream of doing.

On the third day of the twelfth month of our calendar there was another demonstration, in front of a very famous mosque, Pul-i-Kheshtee. The Russians killed three to four hundred people, and more than two thousand people were there to demonstrate. Women and girls and very old people were shot down right in front of the mosque. Even small babies were crying "Allah-o-Akbar!" The Russians kept shooting people down in the streets and on the roofs of their homes. After a week, the Russians had to make the members of one family beg the people to be quiet.

"Allah-o-Akbar," and "Down with KGB. Down with Russia!" "Long live Afghanistan! Long live Islam!" For a week the people called from the windows and from the roofs. Everybody announced what it was they wanted. That was revolution! The skies were full of helicopters and jets, one of which was shot down by one of our freedom-fighters during that week of "Allah-o-Akbar." During the nights, our children became crazy. You could hear shooting constantly, all the time, and every night when we tried to sleep, tanks shook the streets. I was becoming crazy, too, and I thought how much I wanted to be a bird and fly to Moscow and cut Brezhnev's throat.

17

In the province my husband came from, more than six hundred troops and tanks came down the street. When women and children lay down in front of them, the Russians were afraid there were bombs under their bodies, so they stopped the tanks, and the freedom-fighters, who had been waiting for this, attacked them. After this, the Russians were told, "If you see people lying down in front of you, go ahead and drive over them." And they do.

One group of women made a plan to capture some Russian troops in Packtia Province. At the corner of a main road they began to dance when the soldiers came into view. The Russians, thinking it was a wedding or some celebration, assumed it would be easy for them to capture the women and take them to their tanks. But these women had told the freedom-fighters, "When they get out of their tanks and come to see us dancing, attack them!" A lot of tanks and arms were taken: and three or four women were killed.

Every time I thought I might be killed, I told myself not to care. I could teach people through my death that the Russians were killing a lot of women, and show the world what Russians are! I would be grateful for the opportunity to die like this. What else could I do, in my position, without weapons?

For a year I could not make up my mind to leave Afghanistan, but when the government announced that men between the ages of twenty and thirty-five had to sign up with the military, I had to do it. When a truck full of Russian soldiers was sent to take these men away, a woman tried to help one man and called out, "You can't take him!" The soldiers shot her in the chest, then shot her two children, and killed them, too.

You can see my eyes, I cried all last night thinking about my Afghanistan. How much I miss my country and how much I love it! I haven't heard from my parents for four months, and I don't know how they are. But I don't think more about my family than I do about my Afghanistan. At least I have taken my children out of Communism, and I am now ready to die for Afghanistan. Now that I am out, maybe I will have a chance to tell everyone about how bad conditions are for my people. I can read and I can write, and this will be a kind of war against the Russians. That will be useful, too, I think.

In the future I will do whatever I can for my homeland and I

will never let my husband be silent. In the future, when our children go to school and we have found a home, we must always remain Afghan. Because mothers have lost their children, we must remain one with all those Afghan mothers!

Valda Vong, exiled from Phnom Penh by Pol Pot's Khmer Rouge forces in 1976, endured forced labor and near starvation, then fought Vietnamese troops before leading surviving members of her family to safety.

CAMBODIA

When we evacuated out of Phnom Penh, we stayed outside in the jungle a couple of weeks waiting to go back home. For a month, nothing happened. They told us we could take whatever food we could find, so we just took it. Then I saw a lady with a baby in her arms get shot, killed, with two vegetables in her hands. They said she was an "imperialist" because she took what did not belong to her. They said she still had the old way of thinking, so they killed her.

After we were out in the jungle one month, it started raining. Soon we knew there was no way we could return home. We decided to go to my brother-in-law's. It took us about two days' walking, and we had to build a cart to carry our grandparents because they were too old to walk very far. When we got there, it was even worse than before. The people in that area were Khmer Rouge, so it was dangerous for us to be there. We had to register at the village and tell what we had been doing during the last regime. We told them the truth: one sister had finished high school and another was a teacher, and I had been in law school.

The Khmer Rouge said my sister, Vorlerc, was to teach them because many of the Khmer Rouge were farmers and had not been educated. We didn't know then that every time they took someone away like that, they were killed because the Khmer Rouge did not want the educated people to survive.

But Vorlerc came back home in three hours, the only one out of those taken away who returned. She was so lucky. She had con-

vinced them that she had never been in the military, or done anything against the Communists, and they let her go.

We decided then that we had to escape from the village, especially since the Khmer Rouge had warned Vorlerc to say nothing about the others being killed. After midnight, we left and started walking for about twenty-five miles, walking until no one had any shoes left. But it didn't matter how much our feet hurt or how tired we were, we would just cry a little bit and keep on walking.

We got to where we had to cross the Mekong River. There was a big storm, and all was dark. I saw some people sleeping there beside the river on the ground, and they had no food or clothes. Oh, it was so awful to see them, but there was nothing we could do to help. The ground was so bumpy it was hard to move the cart. The rain was falling hard and the ground became muddy and full of rocks. But I knew I had to force myself to go on.

Finally we got to my father's friend's house, but we didn't have any food and there was no place to live. So when it was light I went with my father to find wood to build a house. We thought we had left grandfather asleep, but my grandmother found him dead just after we had gone. She died one month after him, from starvation.

We built a house from wood we found in the jungle. I never worked so hard before, and I pushed myself. We all were overworked and sick from not having enough to eat. Our house was in a section of ten houses with a Khmer Rouge leader. We all had to be members so that we could get food. We didn't care what we ate because we thought we were going to die soon.

If you didn't work, you didn't get rice. We had to stand in water all day, but I felt strong all that time. For women it was all right to eat less than men because men had to work harder, but we got the same amount. So most of the men got sick. At first there were fifteen men in our group, and then only four left alive. First their bodies swelled, and then finally they got medicine which made the swelling go down, but when they were better they got hungry and there wasn't enough food, so they died.

My sister Vannie had a baby only three months old, but because she didn't have enough to eat, she didn't have enough milk to feed him. She was weak with malaria so my mother took care of him. He got skinnier day by day, but then four months later it looked

21

like he was getting a little better. He knew how to laugh and smile and call his mom. Everybody loved him and thought he would get well.

Then one day Vannie had to go to a Communist meeting. When she came back, her baby looked up, smiled, and called, "Mother!" and then he fell back. His pulse had stopped and his breath no longer came. His eyes were still open and he looked like he was still alive. Nobody could believe he was dead. Maybe everything inside him was just too tired.

Vannie's husband died two days before the baby did, and she became like a crazy woman. Her mouth was always closed, she wouldn't talk, wouldn't smile. She felt dead, herself. She told me later that her body stayed alive but that her spirit was dead, buried there with her husband and son.

Five, six months, all that time there was no food. Finally, in December, the fruit started to get ripe, and after it was picked there was still some left on the ground and a few pieces left in the trees. My sisters and I stole it and kept it in a secret place in the forest. I was afraid the Khmer Rouge would catch me stealing and kill me, but I was hungry and had to help feed my brother and father, so I did it. I was not really very scared to die, nobody was because all we could think of was getting our stomachs full.

At that time nobody thought or was afraid of anything. It was like our minds were getting dark, and we could no longer see anything but getting something to eat. We had to eat anything and everything we found in the fields, so many people had diarrhea and other illnesses. They were so weak they had to walk with canes, and most people's hair fell out. We didn't care about things like that, we just thought about surviving.

In 1976, people were terribly hungry. Children of two or three years old ate ants, worms, and dirt when their mothers were away working in the fields. Many died. There was nothing to eat, *nothing*. So sometimes they killed babies to eat. Many babies were dying from starvation, so parents ate them when they died. Some did and others did not, because they remembered the life that was in the child. The mind was dark with hunger.

When people died, we buried them. But in our village there was a man who watched to see where the corpse was buried and then returned at night to cut meat from its legs and eat it. Finally the

Khmer Rouge found out about him and he was killed.

In 1976 we were killed by starvation; in 1977 we were killed by the Khmer Rouge. Mostly the men were killed, but many women were killed also. Sometimes they just pointed at you and said, "That person was a soldier in the old regime," and you would be taken off and killed. The women were all raped first. The leader could rape any woman anytime, but he did it secretly. If you were raped or if you knew anyone who was raped, you just kept your mouth shut.

The Khmer Rouge would kill you if you cried. Not shoot you, but kill you with a bamboo knife, or hit you behind the head, which is worse than just being shot. Often when they killed someone, they cut him open and took out the liver and the bile. The liver they thought would give them strength, and the bile they thought was good for treating malaria. And another thing they did which was really terrible—sometimes they'd cut out the liver and eat it right away, and that kind of person would have eyes like a cat. Always fierce and red, like a tiger.

The liver would be cooked just like cow liver by the Khmer Rouge. It was just meat for them. One of Vorlerc's friends had a brother who was killed, but before he was taken away, his hands were tied and he was led to all the houses in the group. Can you imagine what the sister felt when she saw her brother being led away to die? She was crying inside, but she couldn't cry in front of the Khmer Rouge or they would kill her, too. A while later the leader came back with his liver—and it still moved. It was still alive. He said, "Cook this for me," and gave it to one of the women. She could hardly cut it up because the knife was shaking so hard in her hands. But she had to cut it up, or be killed.

Sometimes they dried the livers and saved them. A family whose son is a Khmer Rouge soldier had a lot of power, especially when he came home with a lot of livers on a stick. They hung them in front of their house and all the people would see it and be afraid.

In 1977, when I was so sick I couldn't work in the fields, they let me do the worst job in the village—collect all the stools for fertilizer. It was a good place for me to be because nobody came near me, and I could hide myself away from the leader's eyes.

We worked 21 hours a day, and then slept in the jungle for two or three hours a night. For a time in 1977 I was gone from my

family for ten months and never knew if they were alive or not. There were fifty of us in our group, but at the end of ten months only fifteen people were still alive. If you didn't work, work, work, they took you away to be killed. I got so hungry! I would pretend I needed to go to the bathroom, and the soldier watching us let me go into the jungle. There I would find leaves and berries I knew were safe to eat because cows ate them, and that was how I stayed alive. I didn't dare take any berries back, because if I was caught eating, I'd be killed.

But I felt strong when I knew I was going back to my family. I walked all day and slept in the jungle at night, and all the way I was wondering if I were really dead. I felt I might be. But as soon as I saw my mother I knew I was alive, and just fell right to the ground. I couldn't sit because I was all bones and it hurt. I was so skinny that nobody knew me. I couldn't take a bath because I couldn't carry the water. I felt like a little tree being pushed back and forth by the wind.

Then, in 1978, they started forcing us to get married, marrying educated people to the farmers. After work we all had to go to meetings, and they taught us how to live the Communist way. Then, they set up two rows of chairs and began to call names, putting the women in chairs in the second row and men in the first row. The man who sat in front of you was going to be your husband. Just like that. You had to leave the mobile group and live with that man in his village. I had good luck that year and they didn't call my name.

When Vietnamese began to fight Cambodians, the Khmer Rouge posted people from the villages up in the jungles to watch the Vietnamese. I heard the bombs of the Viet Cong coming closer day by day, and people left the village for the mountains, forced by the Khmer Rouge to fight or stand guard in the jungle.

A week before the Vietnamese took over, there was another forced marriage ceremony, and then they called my name. "No, even if you kill me right now," I said, "I cannot." I said I would marry when our country was more modern; and that I wanted to join the military and kill Vietnamese. I told a lie. I acted strong, but in my heart I felt terrible. I felt only hate for the Khmer Rouge, but I knew that the only way they would not kill me for refusing was if I could persuade them to think I wanted to fight. It

wasn't only that I didn't want to die, because I would rather have died than to be married to someone I didn't love. If I had children, how could I support them, feed and clothe them?

The Khmer Rouge believed me and I was not killed. They posted me to keep watch in the jungle and help the military. In the daytime I worked in the fields and at night I helped the soldiers. If a soldier had been wounded, I helped carry him in a hammock to the village. One night I brought a wounded man out of the jungle, and after I left him at camp I walked all night to my home. I told my parents, "The Vietnamese are coming closer and they are winning. If they do, you have to go to the city and get help from the Vietnamese soldiers, who will know you are not Khmer Rouge when you ask for help. Don't worry about me. I can escape after you."

In the morning the Vietnamese started bombing and that same night they invaded. They weren't killing anyone and were acting pleasant to us, but I had the feeling that they would be that way only at first. I wanted to escape immediately, but my parents and sisters were afraid. They knew that if the Vietnamese caught people going into Thailand, they'd kill or put them in jail, where they'd starve to death just as they did in the prisons of Pol Pot. We stayed for eight months more, but it was clear that things were growing worse.

I said to my mother, "I'm going with my brother, Sokhom. As soon as we get to Thailand, he'll come back and bring you all over." It was a hundred miles to the border. First we had to pass Vietnamese troops, and then Khmer Rouge forces, and then get by the Thai robbers, who would rape any woman they could. We went on a bicycle, and it took us two days and one night to reach the border. We finally got to an illegal camp on the border, and the next day learned from a Red Cross worker that there was a new camp, a legal one, just opened in Thailand. My brother went back to help the rest of our family escape. "I promise you I'll be back in only one week," he told me, but I waited for him ten days. I cried and cried, but in ten days I saw my whole family arrive. They looked so tired and sick and so very sad. The hospital bus took us right away into Thailand, and as soon as I got on it I felt like floating. I felt, "Oh, my new life looks light again, not dark as it was before."

DOMINIE CAPPADONNA

Dominie Cappadonna, an American social worker, set up holistic medical teams in Cambodian refugee camps on the Thai-Cambodian border for victims of the Viet Cong and the Khmer Rouge.

THAILAND

In October, 1980, the Cambodian exodus started and the newspapers were filled with pictures of starving children. I felt a compelling need to do something. A friend of mine agreed, but we didn't know how to help. We called all the refugee agencies and they all turned us down because we weren't medical doctors. We were both psychologists.

We felt discouraged, and then a Catholic organization called us and said that because it was monsoon season, the refugee camps on the border of Cambodia and Thailand were flooding and babies were drowning. They asked if my friend and I would go over to help set up a camp in the Philippines for children that were thought to be orphans.

It felt like our destiny. My friend and I were apprehensive because of the awesomeness of the task and the newspaper reports telling how terrible things were. We called our friends: a doctor, five nurses, a Catholic nun and a priest, two paramedics, a psychologist and a school teacher. In the space of ten days we wove together a team of fifteen people.

My friend and I had a common vision of a holistic medical team—one that could see people physically, emotionally, intellectually, and also spiritually. While we were developing this different vision of a medical team, we were getting our ten thousand shots and feeling scared to death.

Meanwhile, the United Nations had decided not to airlift the babies because they were concerned that they might actually be

separating families, so our mission was to set up a hospital unit at Khao I Dang, the largest of the refugee camps, with a hundred and fifty thousand people. By the time we got there, there were twenty-two medical teams already established in bamboo huts that housed about a hundred beds. It was a U.N. coordinated effort, so many nations and different religious groups sent teams, as they always do to refugee areas, each with their own specialty. These doctors and nurses on the refugee circuit travel around the world to places where there are crises. It was amazing to me to see that it was kind of an "in group." I had never even considered the politics of it before.

The other teams resented us at first because we didn't look like we fit in. They were mostly A.M.A. types. Some of us are Buddhists and would bow to the people in acknowledgement of their culture and out of respect for them. You should have seen some of the medical teams stiffen and their eyebrows go up!

Our main function in the refugee camp was to care for the emotional trauma cases. Of course, that could have been all the people in camp because everyone was traumatized by famine and all the killings. We knew we had finally gained the confidence of the other medical teams when they started sending us patients who were emotionally traumatized.

We did a lot of simple medical work, and also a lot of holding and touching. We did artwork with people, worked with acupuncture, and reached out to the shamans, the native healers of the Cambodian people, and invited them in. We set up a little spirit house out in front of our hospital; we lit incense and tried in the best way we could to attune our energy to the people we were working with, instead of coming in with our Western psychological viewpoint. The shamans began to come to the hospital with herbs and exorcisms and helped patients that we were having trouble helping.

It was a wonderful experience, meeting needs that weren't being met in other ways. Soon the other medical teams could see that, and our team became a model for all medical teams that go to any refugee camp. We felt grateful that we'd been able to shift awareness of how people can be more fully cared for.

We got very bad press in the San Francisco papers that said,

"They're giving massages and people are dying." But about that time our ward's orientation received support from a Swiss psychiatrist and assistant medical director of the International Red Cross, Jean-Pierre Heigel, M.D., who supported our philosophy of treating the whole person as well as evoking the people's own traditional methods of healing. He was adamant in his concern that the Cambodian people not become psychologically dependent or drug dependent on Western medicine.

These refugees were men and women and families that were coming to us after having walked across Cambodia, starving, and having to decide which children they would take with them and which children they would let die because of the famine. These people had three enemies: starvation, the Viet Cong and the Khmer Rouge. Also, the Thai soldiers could be a threat because Thailand was not entirely friendly with Cambodia. Many women were raped as they came across the border.

We were seeing people who had lost their country, their money, their professions, their clothes, their identification, their food, their families. One thing that deeply impressed me, through all this, was a quality I noticed. Although we as individual human beings may feel our fragility, in the human species, collectively, I saw the human spirit as unsnuffable. In these people who had gone through things that were so awesome and terrible—even through outrageous atrocities—the human spirit lives.

What I was most aware of was that when there's nothing else to lose, what emerges is love and joy and abundance and giving. When I looked at the American team, I saw our neuroses, our pettiness, and I saw how much value the Cambodian people brought to us because of a special kind of freedom they had. There's a real freedom in having nothing to lose. I felt more love being given to me than I think I've ever felt in my whole life, by people who were, in the standards of the world, least able to give of themselves.

On Christmas Eve we were expecting a Vietnamese attack on the camp. Some of the staff were too afraid to work, but somehow I felt no fear. I felt a sense of peace. So I worked the night shift on Christmas Eve. We were making little paper chains, and the kids were hanging them in the bamboo hut. People were dancing and

singing—it was a wonderful display of their culture—and they were teaching their children how to do traditional dances. Some had smuggled their instruments out, and one man had even made a flute out of a bicycle handlebar.

Joan Baez had given us a sewing machine and we had received materials so that we could help the seamstresses make costumes for a big show they were going to put on the next day for the whole camp. Three of us women sewed late into the night, and as the night went on, tension grew throughout the camp. The wind had kicked up and it was blowing the bamboo rushes that were our roof. There was a restlessness in the air, as if any moment the whole thing could explode. I let myself just get in touch with the possibility of all of us being blown up or maimed. I stayed with that thought and let myself see how everyone lying in the hospital, and the hundred and fifty thousand people in the camp had all lived with that quality of tension for months and years, where each moment was alive and with the very threat that the next moment they might be killed. Yet with death so close, they just went about their daily lives.

In the face of this awareness, we had women brought in, three or four a week, who looked like they were in comas. Their husbands brought them in on stretchers. We examined them and determined they hadn't been in a coma, but in a kind of suspended animation. At first, we didn't understand. It turned out to be an hysteric reaction. Their husbands were looking at other women in the refugee camp. Women were feeling possessive, and they had anxiety attacks. It was very touching and quite amazing to me. I had thought that with basic survival at stake, those kinds of things wouldn't happen.

When these kinds of human dynamics were enacted, we did reassuring, "woman" things. As we sewed and cooked together as if we were in our own kitchens, I began to see women as the tapestry-makers of daily life. Part of their ability to survive the loss of their children, the loss of their husbands, survive everything, was to have this kind of activity. We saw women turn around, after being extraordinarily depressed, and begin to make contact again when they had needle and thread in their hands, and they could cook and care for their children.

We had a population that needed to be stimulated emotionally and intellectually too. One of the greatest problems in a refugee camp is ennui, boredom. I have some beautiful examples of shawls women made for me. Giving gifts was a sign of healing because if they felt healed they wanted to do something in return.

There was one woman, a Vietnamese, who had walked all the way from Saigon across Cambodia, and when she got to the Thailand border she was raped by a Thai soldier. She was in our hospital and the thing that worked for her was to give her material to make a shawl. She began to smile and feel she could live because she felt she could mend herself as she sewed the scarf. Another woman came to us because she was having seizures. Medical teams couldn't find anything medically wrong with her, so we felt it was an emotional problem. We had her work with her dreams because Cambodians are very much in touch with their dream life. We got to the issue that her mother, who had died, now in her mind came back as a spirit, and was trying to get her to die and join her. The seizures were a response to feeling pulled over to the other side. We gave her sewing and work that let her reach out and help others. She's still writing to me.

Because of the famine, mothers were forced to choose to let some of their children die. If they made it to the camp with the malnourished baby they had closed off, as well as the healthy child, we had a lot of work to do helping the mother form a new bond with her rejected baby. We had to persuade her that we could help that baby to live. We took the healthy youngsters aside and did artwork or sang with them so the mothers could begin to be with their near-dead children. They had to feel, "My baby's alive."

In many cases the children had to deny a lot just to live. Little orphans were brought to us because they had seen their parents shot. Some children would smile at totally inappropriate times, as if they were in another world, and some children had gone blind because of what they'd seen, they just emotionally stopped seeing. Others looked as if their own childhood made them stronger than the world, and they seemed perfectly natural and normal little kids. Everybody wanted their picture taken, almost as if having a picture of themselves meant that they lived and were preserved in some way, that somebody would know they were alive.

One eleven year old who had seen her parents killed was

severely traumatized, had pneumonia, and no will to live. It was very hard working with her because she wasn't responding. I gave her some art materials and she started to draw. Nothing made sense until the second day when she drew a big butterfly and a flower. In that symbol I knew she had begun to transcend her experience and had decided to live. We've seen the butterfly as a motif in the German concentration camp art of children. It meant metamorphosis, in that they felt they were in a cocoon and would probably die, but understood about life after death. In this case, it showed she had made the decision to live, to come out of the cocoon. It was the light we were looking for.

In older women I sensed a wonderful earthiness—a feeling of their connection with nature and with the land, with their pots of rice and their bare feet on the ground. They were in touch with the rhythm of life. They could cry and express emotion with us, wanted to touch and hug, feel our hair and our clothes. I saw these women keep their families together. These were the survivors, a group that had to be somewhat aggressive in order to live.

Women were easier to help than men. It was more difficult for men to show their emotions, although we had them build structures and other things. We were most concerned about them in terms of boredom and lack of esteem. The women, the ones who were doing the essential tasks and passing on the culture, were healthier. Being responsible for our children, women can't go off the deep end emotionally if there's a child to take care of.

The feeling I came back with was that I really wanted to have a child. I think before I went I had some ethical question about whether I really wanted to bring a child into this chaos. When I saw the strength of the human spirit in that refugee camp, I said to myself, "Of course I want to. I'll do my best to survive." Having experienced the strength of our human aliveness changed my life.

Julie Meissame, an American who married an Iranian, taught in Teheran during the violent rise to power of the Ayatollah Khomeini.

IRAN

When I started college, the women I went around with were all of the same type; all politically offbeat and all studying foreign languages, the more exotic the better. I started with Hebrew, and then Arabic and Persian.

I met my husband in graduate school. He was Iranian and had been studying in the United States for eight years. Just before we got married, he went home on a visit and the first thing they did was to display all the marriageable girls for him to choose from. When he realized what was going on, he told them he was going to marry an American. His mother had a fit and didn't write to him for months, but then I started to write to her in Persian, and she figured out I was a human after all; I could speak the language. It was also a shock to my mother. It took a lot of getting used to, of course.

We lived in the United States, where my daughter Mona was born, for three years before moving to Iran, where we both began teaching at the University of Teheran. To a certain extent my husband changed in Iran into someone I didn't know. Certain aspects of his cultural upbringing caused changes I couldn't have foreseen when we were married, though he didn't change to the degree that some men I knew had changed. Most mixed marriages ended up in divorce because women who were independent and self-sufficient in the States were suddenly told, "No, I don't want you working because my wife isn't going to work. I can support my wife, so you will stay home and do the cooking." Or stay home and talk to his sisters, when none of them could speak the others' language.

I was very fortunate that my husband did not change like that, and that I got along well with my in-laws, which many women did not. My mother-in-law was a very conservative person, religious, well-informed and broad-minded. To me she was always the example of the ideal Moslem woman. One of the most attractive things I found out about Iran, although it could be a bit much sometimes, was the very close family relationships they have in that society. When I grew up I had only my immediate family; just the four of us grating on each other's nerves. No extended family whatsoever. But my husband's family was large and my mother-in-law was actually more maternal than my own mother had been.

Iran was not what I had expected, however. I thought it would be similar to Egypt, where I had lived for a year, but it wasn't. No matter how good my command of the language, no matter how familiar I was with the culture, I never stopped feeling like a stranger all the years I spent there.

Teheran was a very large city with a large, lower-class unemployed population that sort of drifted around the streets. I think the enormous popular support behind Khomeini was that he spoke for the people who didn't dare say anything during the Shah's regime, the underclass who had no say in anything and felt they'd been dispossessed. Many young men who came to the city in search of jobs did not find them and therefore had nothing to do but stand around on streetcorners and resent people who were better off than they were. And if you're a woman who is better off that makes it worse because "women have no right to be better off than men."

It's hard to say how many attacks there were against women because they weren't reported in the press. Most of the incidents I know of were attacks on unveiled women. The fact that a woman is wearing a veil was living proof of male power over her. She doesn't need to be raped, she's already under the male thumb. I think a driving force behind the revolution was the westernization of the culture, especially of the women who were going about unveiled, being educated, entering professions, and becoming more independent. This hostility was very apparent before the revolution, and it came to the fore very dramatically afterwards when laws were passed to enforce the wearing of veils. And it was

33

a fact that the first people to be compulsorily fired from factories and professions and government jobs were women. There were even public demonstrations against women and violence against individual women.

A number of my students were members of the Mujahedin, the left wing Islamic group. One of the ways they protested the Shah's regime was to wear the Islamic headcovering. It hadn't been outlawed but there was a lot of pressure against wearing it, especially in the university, a progressive place. The girls would wear the headcovering or a veil and they could never understand they were being victimized by doing that. They were putting themselves in the position where anybody could tell them what to do because they were showing their own subservience to the male establishment. Now these women are just as politically dispossessed as they were during the Shah's regime.

I found it sad and very difficult to accept that otherwise intelligent women would do this, that they could not see there was no chance of the revolution ever accomplishing anything unless that whole traditional attitude towards women was fought. It has happened elsewhere, "Freedom first, then women's rights." Only you can't have one without the other. You can't have freedom when one half of your population is still not free.

I could see the revolution coming. People became more and more bold about expressing their hostility to people in the streets, especially women and professionals who wore western clothes. I don't think my husband was ever really aware of the hostility against me. I kept trying to tell him how I felt and he would tell me I was imagining things. He was judging only from our circle of friends and family, who were always very cordial and nice.

Nonetheless, I was prepared to live in Iran all of my life. We worked hard to establish a house and a lifestyle that allowed us to live without interference from others, and yet to live in the society and teach and have friends. It was, after a while, a balance between the different areas of our lives. Not perfect, but livable.

During the height of the revolution, we were on sabbatical for a year in the United States. We watched the revolution on television. We'd sit around with a couple of Iranian friends, watching the demonstrations. Then they'd discuss how terrible the Americans were and how they weren't supporting the right people. I told

them I understood what they were saying about the American government, and I felt the same way, but I didn't like it when they'd cast the term "American" in this totally negative way. I always tried not to label a whole people in a negative sense, lumping people together with a government.

When we returned to Iran after Khomeini had come to power, the hostility was very much out in the open. There were demonstrations at the university, and we saw people being beaten up and once several students were shot. There were all these teenagers running around with machine guns, which was unsettling, to say the least. It was frightening because you couldn't predict anything and you never knew who anybody really was or what their motives might be.

There was an attempt to impose compulsory headcovering for all female government workers, and there were demonstrations against this, but eventually the women could only march down a couple of streets before they would be forced to disband, and some women were beaten up. Islamic order was being enforced, in Teheran especially, by mob rule. The Islamic revolution had thought nothing of sending women out in demonstrations where they were liable to get shot by the Shah's army, that was fine. But they didn't end up getting political equality for that!

The religion of the Shi'ite Muslims encourages this kind of violent behavior. They worship martyrs; their big religious holidays mourn people who have been martyred for a thousand years. For these holidays and for funerals, women keep a whole row of black dresses in their closets, because they need to wear black so often. Of course, the chador and the veil are black, so women who wear them look like they're in perpetual mourning anyway. I think all this leads to the feeling in women that their own personal glory can only be achieved if their sons become martyrs. Then they have done something worthwhile, as mothers. Today, boys are volunteering in trainloads to go to the front, kids of fourteen and fifteen, and their mothers are just pushing them onto the trains. In the early days of the revolution, women would dress their small children in shrouds for the demonstrations to show their willingness for their children to die for the cause.

My husband and I began to think about leaving Iran. The main reason we finally decided we must go was the intensifying reli-

gious pressures in the schools. After the revolution they changed the textbooks—rather than the little boy and girl going out shopping together, now the little boy is going to the store while the girl, wearing a headscarf, isn't getting out of the house. I decided there was no way I was going to raise my two girls in an atmosphere where every day of their lives they would be put down for being the "wrong" sex, and never would I permit them to be veiled.

I had mistrusted Khomeini from the very beginning, no matter how much I loathed the Shah, and knew he'd never change after the revolution. The changes he made were, therefore, not entirely unexpected, but quite unbearable all the same. We decided to leave Iran, and my husband resented very much having to leave his country as a result of many difficult circumstances in which we found ourselves. He wanted for a long time to go back. He hasn't gone, but it has been traumatic for him. If the situation there improves in the future, I think he would indeed want to return, but I wouldn't.

One of the things you try to give your children when you come from two different cultures is a sense of themselves as people having a whole lot to draw on. You want to encourage them to see different possibilities open to them. It's not a question of just adopting another culture as your own, but to select what is best from both cultures. Sometimes I think the way to world peace might be to shake up the populations of entire countries by marrying them to each other so they'd have a stake in more than one country's welfare.

Displaced persons surrounded by National police troops at Aguacayo, El Salvador, 1986.

Milena Montano with her great aunt La Conchita who cooks for soldiers in the Nicaraguan mountains, 1981.

Afghani refugees seek shelter, 1985.

A female fighter in the New People's Army in the mountains of southern Philippines, 1986.

*Refugee camp on the Thai-Cambodian border, shelled by
Vietnamese troops, 1986.*

Valda Vong, 1986.

Dominie Cappadonna.

Palestinian women's military training, Jordan, 1970.

Women of the Israeli army during maneuvres in the desert.

40

Republicans, Northern Ireland.

Loyalists, Northern Ireland.

YAEL NADIR

*Yael Nadir, who grew up in an Israeli kibbutz, went into
the army at eighteen for her required service and held an
important job in military intelligence.*

ISRAEL

I grew up in a kibbutz on the north border of Israel. When you
grow up in a kibbutz, you are taught to feel you have to go into
the army and do the best you can for those two years. I finished
school and went into the army, the way everybody else does, at
eighteen.

In the beginning I felt it was a waste of time, but I also felt
really good about giving something to my country, and I knew as
soon as I gave something, I would feel much closer to it. Also, it
turned out to be fun, because I met a lot of new people. A kibbutz
is very small; all the friends you have are the eighteen children in
your class, the ones you grow up with. In the army you have
many more friends, and you get to take care of yourself, a good
change from being protected and dependent in a kibbutz.

I had two months just working on the kibbutz, between gradua-
tion and going into the army, and I felt so free. Then, when I
went into those army buildings, I felt like I was in a place that
was all closed off and I didn't know when I was going to get out.
It seemed like a big deal that suddenly I couldn't do whatever I
wanted. But the army wasn't kindergarten, and you had to learn
to be much more responsible. At first it is like being in a prison
but then, all of a sudden, it becomes your home.

Men and women are separated in the beginning for their basic
training. We learned how to handle guns and did exercises. There
was a lot of laughter about how silly we looked in those big uniforms we were given, carrying those big guns. You can imagine
how I looked with a gun almost as big as I am. I took it all as a

joke, as if it wasn't very serious. One day I put a flower in the end of my gun and an officer came to me and said, "What do you think you're doing?" and all of a sudden it brought me back down to, "Oh, I'm really in the army!" I was just playing like a kid, and it was funny, really, because there was a popular song about putting a flower in a gun for peace—it said that instead of shooting bullets, you should be sending flowers.

I did take the gun lessons seriously, though, because guns are capable of killing somebody. But when we were playing army, I just wasn't very serious. There was no war then, and I probably didn't want to confront the possibility of war. However, I was happy to learn to shoot because I had lived close to the Lebanon border and several times terrorists came into the fields close to our kibbutz. What if I were to go back there and see a terrorist and be unable to use the gun I had? I didn't think about going into war and killing the enemy, but I didn't want to be helpless if I had the opportunity to protect myself and save lives.

There were a lot of hysterical girls, maybe because they had had bad experiences with terrorists, and so didn't want to have anything to do with guns. They weren't forced to shoot them. Our teachers would try to make us feel that we could do it, that we could learn to control our fear about such things. I wasn't afraid. Nothing about basic training was hard for me, mainly because people in a kibbutz get a lot of education about how not to be spoiled. I didn't like the feeling that I was just one person the same as the rest, that I was just one of a whole lot of soldiers, but later on I got used to that and I could see that the soldiers were all individuals in their own way.

I wanted to go into Air Force Intelligence, but they took me into the Military Intelligence of the army. What I had to do first seemed like secretarial work, and I was jittery about just having to sit there and go over papers; but, soon I found it very interesting, and every time a certain place was being discussed as the site of a future mission, I would go to the map and find out where it was. I really wanted to understand exactly what was going on.

It was important work, good work, and the hardest part was not to talk to anybody about it. It's really difficult when you know something is going to happen today or tomorrow and you're excited because you want so much for it to succeed, and you can't

say anything. There was another group that had the responsibility of seeing that nobody said anything about what Intelligence was doing. Part of their job was to find out if I told even my best friend, because a secret between two is not a secret anymore. That is a saying we have in Israel, and it's true.

I felt responsible because many missions were planned in our division. I didn't personally plan them, but I felt I had some responsibility for their success and I was always tense, hoping that everything would go okay. We did what we were ordered to do, and we didn't make mistakes, because if you made a mistake, say, by giving out information, it might kill a whole group of people. You had to be careful because there were a lot of spies around. The army is very smart, but still, an Arab can be spying for you and also spying for the other side. You never know. Arabs mostly work for the money. An Arab who is treacherous because he wants Palestine, that I understand, but to do it just for money, and with no feelings inside?

I knew about quite a few missions, but the most exciting one I knew about was the rescue of our people at the airport in Entebbe, Uganda. The night before the mission we had stayed up very late working out the last details. I finally went home to the kibbutz because there was nothing to do but wait. I sat around with a group of friends, talking. One of the girls said, "I don't know why we're not doing anything!" She was really angry.

I couldn't be quiet, knowing what was to come, and I said in a really innocent way, "How do you know they're not doing anything? Maybe they are, maybe they aren't." She understood right away that something was going to happen, because I was working in Military Intelligence. Some people heard about what I had said, and it was awful. I felt I would have been responsible if something had gone wrong. Several officers came and talked with me and although I could have been put in prison, they understood it was an innocent thing. My boss defended me and said he trusted and respected me, so nothing happened, but I was so scared!

I had some friends who went on the Entebbe mission. I felt it would work because the plans were good and I knew our people knew what they were doing. Because I wanted it to succeed so much, I kept thinking about a successful end and not about the danger. Next day when we went to work we felt proud. It was a

very special time. Of course, we usually do feel strong in Israel, because although we don't have very many people, we're smarter. I don't know how long it will take for Israel to be left in peace, but I know we have the potential to win any fight until then.

I had dreams in the army of participating in war, myself, but when I woke up I never thought I would ever actually fight. There was a study done in Israel in order to find out how capable women would be in a war, and they found out women can stay in war longer, and do many things better because they stay cooler than men. Mentally there is something in a woman that is more calm and quiet that helps her to handle things better. Personally, I think that women who have lost someone can be ferocious with revenge.

As for how we feel about the Arabs, I don't know how it is we got prejudiced against them as we were growing up. Maybe from the army, or maybe because of the wars. There were many times we didn't go to school because of the terrorists nearby. We knew they were coming to destroy us, to kill as many people as possible, and I saw what they did. I had friends who were killed—but then it's like anyone you know who dies; it hurts, you miss them, and then you start getting used to them being gone, you start to accept it.

Very close to the kibbutz there was a bus full of children going to school, and a bomb from Lebanon destroyed it. It was shocking, I couldn't understand how they could do that! What you want to do immediately is to take a gun and go kill the somebody responsible for such terrorism. But after a while you cool down, you change. That day passes and you just don't want to think about it anymore. The feeling of revenge is in a not-aware part of us that makes us angry without good reason. It isn't rational at all.

But a terrorist comes and he knows exactly what he's going to do. He's coming with the premeditated purpose of killing. I cannot accept how someone can just take somebody else's life. I guess when it's war, you're working like you are a machine, and you don't think about the people you are killing.

I was happy when I finally got out of the army, very happy. But it was hard to decide then what to do. In the army you think all the time about what you're going to do when you are free and

there will be nobody to tell you what to do, and then, when you're out, it's a shock to suddenly have all these possibilities. Then you have to learn to make choices.

All I was sure of when I got out of Intelligence was that I wouldn't do that kind of work again! Still, in the beginning, it was hard not to know what was happening. It wasn't enough for me to know only what the radio said. I'd call the office every once in a while just to find out what was happening. They didn't tell me everything, but if it was something I had known about when I was with them, they'd give me a hint. It was funny how helpless I felt all of a sudden. Before, I had had a lot of power. I really knew what was going on . And then, after a while, I got used to not knowing.

ANAT TABORI

Anat Tabori volunteered for the Israeli air force and saw action in the Gaza Strip during the Yom Kippur War in October, 1973.

ISRAEL

War didn't mean very much to me growing up. It seemed very distant, and Israel seemed somehow isolated from dangers. Then a neighbor and some friends of the family were killed in the Six Day War, and that was my first inkling that war can have such a great effect on one's life. I remember being overwhelmed with fear. However, I think I dealt with that fear by ignoring it and trying not to worry about it.

When I was about to be graduated from high school, and was dating the man who would become my husband, I got much more involved in politics and how they influenced events in our country. I changed very much through this awareness and spent my energies on trying to learn as much as I could about what was going on, and then trying to see the other side and to work through solutions, which I thought I had at eighteen.

I went into the army, like all Israeli eighteen year olds. It was a secure time; it was my first experience away from home and my parents, which was exciting. I joined the part of the army that historically was set up to create settlements along the borders for the purpose of protecting the country.

Women went through harsher basic training in that part of the army than women in other parts because it was felt we had to be prepared to defend the settlements and do more physical work. We trained with the men and were expected to do much the same thing. We handled the same weapons and studied the same theories and skills. I already had a premilitary course in high school, which was required for all students with the idea that if there

47

should be a war, men would go to the Front and women should be able to help protect the population. The course had included a weapons class which scared me at the time. But once I got into the army, having a gun over my shoulder seemed entirely natural.

Basic training was two or three months, and the rest of the six months we spent on a kibbutz in preparation for building our own settlement. We learned how to live communally and to be independent in all the different components of kibbutz life. But I wasn't happy with what I was doing. I knew I had the ability, the skills and the intelligence to contribute more to the army. I was also motivated to see different things and meet different people; and I really wanted to be in the Sinai, not where I was up north, in the Golan Heights. The Sinai seemed a very romantic place to me, exciting and different.

I left my unit after six months and went to the army placement center. It was decided that I should be placed as a secretary about five minutes from my parents' home, which was my first confrontation with being put in a stereotypical woman's role. I was furious and determined to fight it. I used every influence I could think of. I went in and talked to any officers who would listen to me, but none of them were any help. I told them I wasn't leaving the building until they found a better situation for me, and they sent me to talk with a psychiatrist.

I told him, "Look, I want to go to the Sinai. I'm a perfectly normal individual and I know exactly what I want. Help me, and I'll be out of your office." He did, and it worked. I really think there were a fair number of women who wanted to be more than clerks or secretaries, but not all of them were as persistent as I was. There was always the feeling that women were in the military to support the men, that men were fighting the war and women were just there to help out. I could never really accept that.

They told me I could be in the Air Force and go to the Sinai, and I was exhilarated. At that time, in 1972, the Sinai was relatively secure, with only occasional attacks and terrorist incidents, and my parents and boyfriend and I were not concerned about my going there. As a woman I was given a high-responsibility job, and I was impressed they had given it to me. Still, if I'd been a man, I could've done much better.

After completion of my training, I was stationed at a rather iso-

lated Air Force base at the most southern part of the Sinai Penin-
sula, which I thought was wonderful. The work was difficult. I
was with Intelligence and learning different codes and how to
identify airplanes. I was using my mind and felt I was learning
something very important, things that other people didn't know,
which gave me a feeling of power.

It was a wonderful time to interact at an intense level with other
men and women. I found out that I was good at adapting to
whoever was around. I also developed the ability to be alone in
the middle of a crowd, to isolate myself.

There was some talk of Egyptian soldiers trying to cross the
border and infiltrate our bases in order to kidnap people they
could use as ransom, and that was scary. When that information
was passed down we wouldn't go anywhere outside the unit,
unless we were going in a military jeep and, as always, had our
machine guns with us.

I was home on leave the day the Yom Kippur War broke out,
and I returned to my unit the very next day. Although we were
not a fighting unit, more of a protective Intelligence unit, we had
all these antennas that attracted a lot of attention, and the Egyp-
tians bombed us soon after the start of the war. All of the communication lines broke down between our unit and the other
military units around, which to us was no big deal. We didn't
realize what that meant, and only later did we find out that everyone else thought our unit had been wiped out.

We did suffer casualties. Coincidentally, all of them were men.
Fortunately so, according to reports by the military, who didn't
feel good the men died, of course, but felt, "What would our army
look like if women died?"

We kept right on working, just as if nothing had happened, and
it wasn't until seven weeks later when I got home and began talking to people that I realized how serious the situation had been
and what could potentially have happened. I have never really
come to grips with exactly how I felt during the hours of the
bombing. On a rational level I knew we were in danger. We were
isolated, and I knew that, as women, we were in some danger of
being sexually attractive objects to the enemy, but still I felt I was
in control and could take care of myself.

Not only did our side assume we had all been killed, but the

enemy assumed the same thing, so they ceased the attack. We weren't allowed to turn on any lights at night, and it was frightening to be in that darkness, not knowing if everyone around you was supposed to be there or not. But I didn't let that fear, or any other emotion, come to the surface.

All of the men killed had been good friends of mine, and I felt very confused when I heard about their deaths. I lived with what had happened, and went on with my job. I remember thinking, "Why don't I feel terribly depressed, terribly lost? What is wrong with me?" I was afraid I was getting calloused by the war, turning into a machine with no feelings. That disturbed me. I was acting just the same as everybody else, men and women, doing our work and socializing in the evening the way we always had. From time to time we'd mention what had happened and feel depressed about it, but then we'd get over it really fast. It was as if there were a nonstated agreement that we shouldn't dwell on it.

I felt divided in two, the little girl who was brought up to be feminine, to worry about everybody else and to have all these emotions; and then there was the real me, who had been brought up by the army to be self-confident and to deal with real-life situations, to expect them to happen and live on after they did. These two parts of myself were in conflict, and they fought each other continually. I recognized some of that conflict at the time, but the stronger me won out over the stereotypically female behaviors.

There was a tremendous amount of internal strength that I didn't realize I had but was pulling up from somewhere inside of me. Indeed, I did have the strength to deal with war in a very healthy way, but at the time it didn't seem that I was dealing with it with my female strength. It has been a problem all my life, a common problem for women, that I didn't have real strong role models. So I ended up looking up to the men, trying to feel and respond the way they did. Now I know that I should create my own role models.

By this time my boyfriend had been in the army for some time, and though I had really liked him before he was in the army, it was only after he joined that I truly grew to love him. Sometimes he'd come home on leave when I was also on leave, wearing his dirty uniform and his gun hanging from his shoulder, and it was the ideal macho image for me. I remember thinking there was

something wrong with that feeling, but I never pursued it.

I felt the fear and jealousy about the women in his unit, and I still do. But I never felt sexual jealousy, which makes me feel very good about myself as a feminist. I almost assumed there was a fair amount of sex that went on, as it did in my unit also, but that didn't bother me. What worried me was that he would get involved in a close emotional relationship that would mean more to him than the relationship he had with me. I suspect he was jealous of me, too, although he never said so.

I ended up seeing a great deal more of the war than my husband did. He wasn't jealous of me for that, but at the time he was frustrated and upset. In Israeli society, if you are not part of the war you are in the wrong place at the wrong time. My greater involvement didn't affect our relationship, though, and just like every other area in life, he was a constant source of support for me. The army was a great equalizer in our relationship. We have a common history and we have common terms.

When the war was over, and the two years of my military service ended, I wanted very much to go home. It took me a short time to realize that I could never go back home and be comfortable again as somebody's daughter. The army had made me too independent for that. There were things I began to miss, and sometimes still miss, about the army. It had been two years of my life in which I didn't have to make decisions because the army had made them all for me. I was told what to do and I could bitch about it, but I had to do it. Day and night we complained.

My boyfriend and I got married, and then the subject of children came up. I want very much to have children, even though I worry about bringing children into a world where they might get killed or their parents might die in war. I guess more than anything I hate the idea that we will be having children who must go to war. All that time I was growing up, it was very obvious to me that I would be in the army, but now it's disconcerting to me that my children will be growing up with that same attitude. It creates an undesirable predisposition for having war, and an acceptance of war. In Israel we really do bring up our children to go to war.

And yet, it's almost as if my experiences have taught me that you have to go on living. And I want the joy of having children in that life. It is conceivable I could live somewhere safer to bring up

children, but I don't want to. Israel is my home and my country. There is a certain bond I feel to the land and to the people, a bond that would never let me establish a life elsewhere.

I am also terribly frightened by the idea of being a widow. At this time inequality has it that I will not go into fighting, but my husband will, if there is another war. Actually, I think it would be easier for me if I were to go instead of him, although that's an easy thing to say. But it's a frustrating feeling to have no control whatsoever over what would happen.

When I was eighteen I had all the solutions. I felt that Israel should be very compromising and that we should do anything in the world to obtain peace. Now I have the same feeling; however, I also get the feeling we could do everything in the world, and still we would be at war. Nonetheless, if I truly believe that I want children to live in peace, then I can't say that the hatred between Israelis and Arabs will continue forever. I must believe that it will not—that there is a way out and that things will get better.

NUHA NAFAL

Nuha Nafal, a member of the Palestine Liberation Organization who lived in Jordan during the twelve days of Black September violence, 1970, went into exile in the U.S. after her country was occupied by Israel.

PALESTINE

I was born in 1943 in Berziet, ten miles north of Jerusalem, four years before the war. So I was four years old when the refugees first came to our town when the tragedy started. A year later, my mother told me to put black sheets over the windows and to stay close to home because the streets might no longer be safe.

My mother was a wise and capable woman. My father had died before I was born and so she raised me and my three sisters with money she made from her sewing. She would advise people about their troubles and she had a deep feeling for helping others. When the refugees came she opened our house to them and made them welcome, telling them, "Stay here. This may be your home until you can go back to your own."

Five families stayed with us. Our house was very large but it had only one room. Several families stayed in the corners of the room and another family lived downstairs where the animals were kept, sleeping in the empty stalls. There must have been twenty-five or thirty people in addition to my own family; and some people even had to live on our roof during the summer when it was very hot.

At first my sisters and I were upset, and we kept saying to our mother, "But where shall we sleep? You gave them our beds and we are tired." She whispered to us, "Be easy, it will only be for a week or so, at the most a month, and everyone will go home again." We had to sleep on the floor in a corner beside our mother, without a bed and without privacy for four years! When I

asked my mother, "Why do these people have to stay in our house?" she told me, "Because Israel took away their lands, and they have no homes."

I felt bitterness because of that, and anger. I do not like to speak of hate, but I felt hatred too. I started to ask myself, what kind of people were those who would kill my people and expel them from their lands? I asked my mother, "But we were living peacefully together. We were coming and going as we wished, and all of a sudden what has happened?" There was no answer to that. No one could believe it at first, and then we kept thinking the hostilities would be over soon and everyone could return to their lands. Ten years passed, then fifteen, and now it is thirty-five years later and still we are homeless, stateless, without identity. Through the years our bitterness has increased.

It was a time of poverty, homelessness and sorrow. I felt homeless, too, even in my own home, because the refugees who lived with us were occupying my house. I knew we were in the middle of a bad problem, but I didn't really understand why it had had to happen to us, changing our lives so suddenly, so completely. Even now, sometimes, I feel lost and depressed. I get heart palpitations and a kind of anxiety that I do not know how to stop, it seems so unconscious and out of my power to control. I don't like to be emotional about it, but it hurts so much to remember. It wasn't as bad for me, of course, as it was for those people from the first part of Palestine to be occupied. They came with nothing, with only the feeling they would soon be able to return home. They had all kept their house keys with them. My brother, who had come to us from Jaffa, would say to me, "Do not lose the key to my house, whatever you do. We will need it when we go home to Jaffa." It was kept on the top of a cupboard, and I would go to look at it from time to time, and think of the beautiful city I had never seen. The city I would never see.

We really did not feel so bad for ourselves when the others talked about what had happened to them. One of the refugees had left her baby on the bed, and when she had had to flee so quickly she grabbed up the pillow instead of her baby and ran away. She would cry and cry and say to us, "I want to go back for my baby! What if he has been hurt? I must go back!" It is a picture I cannot

forget, that woman sobbing so helplessly for her child.

After a time we were under the jurisdiction of the Jordanian government which separated the refugees into large groups and gave them land to build tent camps in Palestine, Jordan or Lebanon. They lived there one, two, three years .... After a while no one could imagine how long it would be before they would be allowed to go home. Some of them were still in the tent camps of Shatilla and Sabra at the time of the massacre in 1982.

The United States started sending clothes through the missionaries, and the Red Cross started helping out. Many organizations began to give refugees food and milk, but you can't imagine what it was like in those tent camps in winter! Small children were without shoes, without enough food, freezing. They grew up feeling they wanted to fight to get their homeland back, the gardens they had played in, the life they had once known.

In 1948, eighty percent of the Palestinians were forced to give up their lands, but it wasn't until 1967 that my family in Berziet was also forced to give up our land. When it looked like the Zionists would occupy all of Palestine, the Palestine Liberation Organization was formed. From that time on we started to understand the conflict and to join forces, but by 1967, as we were spread out all over the Middle East, we did not have the power to resist the Israeli forces.

Even at that time, we were not as understanding about the refugees and their suffering as we should have been. We still looked down on them as second-class citizens. They were the refugees while we were the owners of the land they were camping on. We could not then believe that we would soon be refugees, too. But then, in 1967, there was the tragedy of the Three Days' War, and all of our land was occupied. All of us were refugees then. No one knew that once we had left our city we could never return for our furniture or money or whatever else we possessed.

By this time I was married and my husband and I went to live in Aman, Jordan. There was a bridge between Jordan and Palestine, and you had to have permission from a relative in Israel and the Israeli government in order to visit. You had to stay on that bridge twelve to fifteen hours before being allowed to enter. First they searched all our bags and made us take off all our clothes and

be x-rayed to see if there was anything hidden in our bodies. Our clothes went into another room, our shoes were sent somewhere else to be checked, and our bodies were put through a machine. The woman in charge had her feet up on her desk and a cigarette hanging from her mouth and talked to us like we were animals! The Zionists talk about human rights, but of course, the Zionists never considered us to be human beings.

The next tragedy came in 1970 with the Black September fighting between the Palestinian guerrillas and the Jordanian Army, when Jordan tried to expel our army because they were afraid of what Israel would do with them on its border. It was more of a tragedy, really, because it was Arab against Arab.

With two of my children, I struggled to survive the twelve days of fighting in a section of the city under the control of the PLO. My house had one room and sometimes there were twenty-five people in it. The children had no food and almost no water. After five days, no one had anything at all—no food, no electricity. They killed hundreds of us as they tried to expel our soldiers from the country.

I felt I had to help my people as much as I could, so I tried to feed our soldiers when they came to us for help, or give them a place to hide from the Jordanian army. It was hard because there were few of us and the army was strong. I suppose that going out into the streets to hunt for food was dangerous, but the moment you are doing something like that you cannot allow youself to feel the danger. I didn't think too much about my life. I was eight months' pregnant at the time, but the need to help my people was my strongest feeling.

My kitchen was built into the rocks of a hillside and that is where we went to protect ourselves from bombs or machine-gun fire. Neighbors would come hide in my house during the bombings if they didn't have anywhere safe to stay, so there were many of us. One day while we were crowded into the kitchen side of the room, one wall across from us was hit by a bomb and everything near the wall was destroyed as well.

The day after the Black September was over, I left on the first plane out of Jordan with only my two children and the dirty clothes on our backs. Thousands of Palestinians were waiting at the airport to ask us about their relatives. It was so wonderful to

see them all! I felt like we were all one people, and no matter how far we had been divided from each other, we were still one hand helping the other.

I am angry when I hear the PLO described as "terrorists." We are not terrorists. We want our legitimate rights, and that is all our army is fighting for. We want peace, but a fair peace that gives us the right to live in our homeland in freedom and dignity, and not under control of Israel. I believe in my heart, because I must, that someday we will regain Palestine and rule ourselves.

Many women feel as I do and are in the PLO. If we had the freedom to do so I think eighty percent of Palestinian women would go to the Middle East and fight. After all, we have suffered more than the men. When a soldier dies, he is dead. But who is still suffering? The mother. The sister. The wife. And a woman is usually more emotional than a man and has stronger feelings, which only increases her determination to kill an enemy who killed her son. But it is difficult still for women to go and fight. What is standing in the way is our culture. A woman's husband would feel that he should be the one to fight and the wife should stay at home to take care of the children.

That was a problem for me. I used to attend meetings of Palestinian women and get back late at night, so late that my husband and children would be worried and upset. After thirty or forty times, I did as they wished and quit going. I was depressed because I felt I was needed to teach the women who were not as politically passionate as I am. Palestinian women have more freedom than women in most other Arab cultures, but still it isn't easy for us to talk openly about our feelings. But I think the Palestinian cause forces women to ignore things that would try to stop us. From 1948 on, we have struggled and carried guns and fought beside male soldiers. Many Palestinian women have been in Israeli jails as political prisoners since 1967. The women in the PLO are guerrillas doing everything a man can do, but they are usually not married or they are divorced because they refused their husband's request to stay home.

I am ready to fight whenever I am asked to do so. It is also all right with me if I have to send all my four children, even if they were to die helping their people. My daughters as well as my sons can fight. When the Beirut massacre happened, I said to them, "If

you would like to go to Lebanon and help, then go." But they were underage and not allowed. However, when they are old enough, I will go along with them and fight by their side. They have already seen many of our friends and relatives leave for the Middle East, and several of them have been killed. We feel their loss deeply, but we are aware the struggle will take the death of many.

Sometimes I am depressed and anxious, and at other times I feel strong and full of hope that we are getting stronger and that there will be a Palestine. Often there are applications and documents to fill out and always there is the question of where one is born. What pain I feel from that simple question. In 1943 it was Palestine, but when the application is returned, Palestine is always crossed out and Israel written in, instead. At first I was so upset I could not sleep at night, being forced to deny my nationality, my home; but now, I write what they wish and I say nothing. But I am Palestinian. My hair is Palestinian, my body is Palestinian, and the words I speak are Palestinian. My death will be Palestinian!

GEORGINA GORDON

Georgina Gordon saw her Loyalist husband and their two children blown up by a bomb planted in the family car by Republicans.

IRELAND

I've lived in Maghera, County Londonderry, all my life. I was a housewife with three children, and my husband was a social worker who joined part time with the security forces organized as a peacekeeping measure in Northern Ireland. His job was to check out vehicles for concealed bombs and then deactivate them.

On the morning of February 8th, 1978, my husband came down to take our two oldest children to school. He went out to check the car, which was something he had to do all the time. They had put the bomb right up into a cavity in the car, and he didn't find it. The ironic thing was that my husband was a very keen fisherman, and they had connected invisible fishing line to it.

He got into the front seat beside my daughter, and my eight year old son, Richard, got into the back. I had my three year old daughter, Lindsay, in my arms when I went to the window to wave them off.

The car was right in front of the window when it exploded. The shock of the impact left me motionless, unable to see or hear anything, and it was only my child talking about the smoke and broken glass that made me realize what had happened. When I got outside the car was completely torn apart. My husband and daughter were still sitting in the front seat, but their legs were badly cut up and I thought they were unconscious. Richard was not in the car, and I realized he had been thrown out of it by the blast. He was lying across the road. He was badly burned, his face and legs had been slashed with shrapnel and pieces of metal were still in his legs. He was covered with blood.

They were taken to the hospital. Some time later the minister and a friend came to the house, and the minister was crying. He told me that my husband and daughter were dead, and that Richard had been taken to the Royal Victoria Hospital, fifty miles away.

By the time I went up the following morning, Richard had had an emergency operation and was in Intensive Care. I was told not to discuss the bombing with him. We kept off the subject as much as we could, but he was very bright in his mind, even then, and he wanted to know how his father and Leslie were. I told him they were in another hospital.

The bombing was on Wednesday, and on Saturday the two funerals took place. Sunday morning I went to the hospital and one of the nurses took me to one side and said that Richard had kept asking for his Dad. I decided we had to tell him, in the most humane way possible. He was quiet for a moment, and then he said, "But why *Leslie*, Mommy? Why not me?"

Richard spent seven weeks in the hospital. There was a lot of skin grafting to be done, and I was his only donor. During this period, Lindsay was having terrible nightmares. The doctor prescribed sedatives for her, but I decided to let her talk it out.

When Richard came home on crutches we had a celebration, but Lindsay refused to believe her dad and Leslie were not in another hospital. That refusal went on for about two years.

At first, especially when I thought the terrorist might be someone I knew, I felt very hurt. I had delayed shock, and though it was terrible, it wasn't possible to break down in front of the children. If I had to cry, I'd go in the bathroom, turn on the taps, and let go.

Richard lost the sight in one eye and very nearly lost the sight in the other. His legs are mending, but he's still having operations on his ears. He can't swim or be in school sports, but he's very brave about that. He will not talk about the bombing, but Lindsay recounts every detail when she is feverish. I see the car exploding before my eyes every time I look out the window. I see it happening, no matter where I am, again and again, all the time. It has shattered us. As someone in the security force, my husband wore a uniform and was out in the open. They could easily have

shot him. Instead, they decided to do what they did. They had it planned, premeditated. Now, if you asked the terrorists why they did it, they'd tell you he shouldn't have been in the security force in the first place. Very well, but tell me—what about my children?

SUZANNE BUNTING

Suzanne Bunting was severely wounded by two terrorist gunmen who broke into her home and killed her husband, a Republican sympathizer.

IRELAND

My husband was a Republican sympathizer and an executive of the National H Block Armagh Committee, working to help political prisoners who were being treated like common criminals. There had been other political figures killed, including a forty-five-year-old woman, shot four times in the head in her own home. Ronnie became very aware then that he could be a target, too. He was careful during the day, and no one in the Nationalist areas will open their doors at night until they know who is there knocking because the government won't give you a license to own a weapon, even if it is for your own self-protection. If they search your house and find a weapon, it means ten years in prison. So we didn't have one. We were sitting ducks.

A friend was staying with us, sleeping in the baby's room. Our two other children were in the back bedroom. For security precautions, we had a bolt on our bedroom door, but we always left it open because of the children. Sometimes they got upset at night and wanted to come in, and we didn't want them to feel closed out. At the time, they were just seven and three years old, and fifteen months.

It was about 3:30 a.m., and we were asleep. We were awakened by a loud banging on the door. Two gunmen used a sledge-hammer to smash the front door in. Ron and I tried to rush to the door to put the bolt on, but one of the gunmen was already there, pushing to get the door open, while we were pushing to shut it. It's hard to judge time, it was probably only seconds, and then shots were fired. One man had gotten his gun around the door.

He shot my hand, and I fell backward onto the bed.

I knew that Ronnie had no chance; he wasn't armed against the two gunmen who were standing there at the door wearing ski masks. I knew he was going to be killed. I didn't want to have a picture in my mind of Ronnie being shot; I didn't want to live with that picture for the rest of my life, so I turned away and rolled up in the bed so I wouldn't see it. There was nothing I could do to stop it.

I expected one or two shots, but there were so many that I looked up to see what was happening. One of the gunmen was standing over my husband's body continually pumping it with bullets. He was shot nine times. I *had* to stop them. I jumped up and grabbed the gunman by his back. He tried to reach around with his gun and shoot me, but I had such a strong grip because of my panic, gripping like death, that he couldn't get me off.

The other gunman, who was standing at the top of the stairs, shot me twice then, once through the shoulder and once under the arm. I fell back; I couldn't hold on to him anymore. They backed out of the room and I looked down. I could see Ronnie was dead; his eyes were open, staring, and his body was so white. I fell back, leaning against the wall at the top of the stairs so that I wouldn't fall, and as the gunmen went on down the stairs, one of them said, "Come on, Geordie, hurry up," and he lifted his gun and shot me in the mouth.

I lost part of my tongue, the teeth were all gone in that side of my mouth. The bullet hit my spine, and there was permanent damage, and I can't move my neck very far anymore. The blood was running down my throat into my lungs and it was instinctive to get the blood up. I knew I would drown if I didn't. I turned around on my knees and bent over, facing the baby's room. I could hear him screaming—he'd watched the whole thing. Ronnie had been shot in front of his room, and he'd seen me shot.

The baby was in hysterics. After the gunmen had left, my two girls came up behind me, screaming. My eldest girl, who was seven, has a very strong character. She kept saying, "Mommy, what can I do? What can I do?" I tried to tell her to go get help, but I had to say it three times before she understood what I was saying. Her father's body was lying halfway out the bedroom door

and across the top of the stairs and she had to climb over it to get out.

She brought the neighbors and they took all the children away and called for an ambulance. That was eighteen months ago.

The children kept me going to a large extent, because I had to keep a brave front with them. When they caught me crying they would get really upset, so I had to keep the grieving to myself. I had to see that we returned to everyday life. There is no alternative, if you have children.

PEGGY TUXEN AKERS

Peggy Tuxen Akers served in Vietnam as a nurse in combat-zone intensive care units. She has returned her Bronze Star and is fasting with other veterans to protest U.S. government policy in Central America.

VIETNAM

The army paid my last two years of college, so I owed them time. I've always been sort of a rebel, but when I was sent to the six weeks' basic training at Fort Sam Houston, I decided I was not going to buck the system. I was going to wear the uniform the way they wanted and toe the line and make the six weeks as much fun as I could.

After basic training I got orders to go to Vietnam. In a way I guess I volunteered to go there. I mean, I didn't try to find a way not to go. In some ways I wanted to go, but I'm not even sure why.

When I first got to Qui Nhon, they took us through all the wards, including the intensive care unit, where I ended up working the whole time I was there. I looked over at one patient and he seemed familiar to me, so I looked at the chart on the end of his bed and found that he was a friend from my hometown whom I had played with as a child. He was totally blown up. I couldn't believe it was him. I remember running out of the ward and puking my guts out. Here I was, this idealistic nurse gone in to help soldiers, and suddenly it struck me that it was fucked—the whole thing! These were people's bodies. Everything felt different to me from that moment on. I knew then that it wasn't at all what I'd thought it was going to be.

I was pretty patriotic. My parents were immigrants from Denmark, and they thought America was wonderful and they flew the flag every Sunday. I was co-captain of the cheerleaders and would always walk in the parades. But then, after seeing my childhood

friend, that kind of patriotism suddenly seemed crazy.

I had been involved in protests against the war at college, but I still kept some idealism about our country. Part of me still feels guilty about going to Vietnam, because we learned in basic training that in a war the first people to go in are the aids to scope the place out, but the next to go in are the medical people to set up the hospitals and M.A.S.H. units. I felt that if all of us "intelligent people," those of us who have a deep respect for human life, had said, "No, we're not going over to Vietnam, we're not going to support this war, it's wrong," then it would never have lasted. But I suppose it doesn't ever work out that way.

I am glad now that I went over because I'm a good nurse and I cared a lot, and I feel I helped save a lot of people's lives. The situation was very different from World War II. In Vietnam there were modern helicopters with great pilots, and as soon as there were casualties, they would fly into the most harrowing weather or into combat to pick up the wounded and bring them right to the hospitals. We'd get them fresh from the field and save their lives. We were fixing these people up to send them back to get killed. It was crazy, awful. I wanted them to live, but I didn't want them to get well enough to go back in. Of course, I was in the intensive care unit where 99.8 percent never went back in; they either died or went back home—with no arms, no legs, no brain ....

It isn't fair for me to say what "we as nurses" felt, because I'm not sure what other nurses were feeling, but when I was taking care of the G.I.s I felt I was really important to them, that I was the one contact they had with their whole life back home. When they woke up, they saw us nurses there, looking like their sisters or wives; there was nothing sexual about it at all. So I tried to be all those things for them, tried to be their sister or mother and do those things that they would do.

It was important, of course, that these men be in touch with reality and not really get us confused with people back home. But it comforted them to be reminded of someone they loved, and it was always really easy for me to touch and hug and hold them, because that kind of warmth has always been important to me, too.

We had wounded Vietnamese, too, and taking care of them was

66

no different to me than taking care of the G.I.s. That wasn't true for all the nurses, and a lot of American soldiers didn't like to be in bed next to a Vietnamese, even though we were fighting on the same side! Anytime you heard a helicopter, you knew casualties were coming in—even to this day when I hear a helicopter my stomach turns—and the emergency room would have been notified already about how many wounded were Vietnamese or G.I.s. If they were Vietnamese, nobody moved very fast. And there were kids, little Vietnamese kids we took care of after their bodies had been blown apart. Their parents would come to sleep under their beds at night. The stupid army rules wouldn't allow that, but we'd sneak them in at night to be with their children. It was a crazy war in that respect.

When we had to make priority decisions about medicines and respirators, about who was going to live and who was going to die, the G.I.s always came first. I'm not saying that was wrong, but I really feel bad that decisions like that had to be made at all. There were always plenty of guns and bullets! There was no reason why there couldn't have been enough medicine or plasma or suction machines. We should never have had to choose. I hated it when I had to make those choices.

We were always busy. I don't think people understand what nurses went through over there. Some nurses at the Veterans Administration are beginning to speak out, but nurses are basically not very outspoken. Nurses are women and women are the nurturers, and we were the women over there.

People worked really hard and played really hard. When I first got to Vietnam, I couldn't believe how much people drank and smiled and laughed. It disgusted me. I just couldn't believe that after people had dealt with death and dying all day they could party. Soon I realized it was impossible to get through a whole year in Vietnam spending all your time crying, though that's what I did at first.

I was lucky that at Qui Nhon I met Jim, who was a medic. He was married, and he became like a very close brother to me. We'd go for walks, and both of us used to go to a leper colony, run by French nuns along the South China Sea. We'd help out with the orthopedic surgery, amputations and suturing, and because I knew French, I could translate between the nuns and the doctors. I

usually went there during the day when I was on the night shift. It was beautiful there, and the nuns would cook a wonderful meal for us, made from what they grew in their own garden. It was such a change from eating canned stuff in the mess hall. We'd do surgery for a couple of hours and then go swimming for a while. It was a place where Jim and I could walk along the beach and talk. He told me all about his wife and his life back home. I felt really close to him, but I knew on some level that if our friendship became sexual it would be ruined, and that our friendship was the most special thing I had.

Everyone drank a lot because we were under such pressure. I think the only reason I didn't was because I was afraid I could get hooked on the escape of alcohol. I don't think I'm unusually strong, but I do think I'm a survivor. I know how to take care of myself, and that included not drinking and not getting involved in relationships that were going to end up hurtful. When I got transferred and had to say goodbye to Jim, it hurt, but it wasn't a tremendous loss for me. I had protected myself from feeling loss. Even when patients died, I didn't fall completely apart. I think on some level I didn't let myself feel more than I could stand, and I was afraid that if I drank I might've felt too much.

I got transferred to a much more dangerous hospital, up at Chu Lai. We were on red alert all the time. I spent many hours under beds with patients on respirators, caring for those who had had tracheotomies and couldn't breathe without help. Under the Geneva Convention, hospitals are protected, but there was fighting all around us and the lights were all off and we had to wear flak jackets and helmets and do our work by flashlight. Sometimes we'd have patients who couldn't be moved, and all we could do was put a mattress over them to protect them. One nurse got hit by shrapnel from a bomb that exploded outside. It hit her in the jugular and she bled to death. Nurses were killed in Vietnam, though according to the V.A., they were killed in helicopters on joyrides, which is a lie.

When I came back from Vietnam, I was interviewed a couple of times, but no one ever asked me what it was like in the war. People don't want to know, I guess. One reporter asked if I cried in Vietnam. I said, "Yes, but I stopped. I couldn't constantly grieve."

But the headline of the article turned out to be, "I Never Cried!" I was furious.

I didn't talk much about Vietnam for a while, but not talking about it only made me feel worse. It got to where I had to talk about it with someone, because I was ready to fall apart. I went to the vet center, and the facilitator in charge said to me, "When do you want to start volunteering?" I said, "I'm not here to volunteer. I'm here because I'm hurting and I need help. I need to talk with someone." Well, he'd never met a woman vet before. No one had.

He invited me to attend a meeting of a rap group. I came in on the first night and the vets were sitting in a circle. I told them who I was. I wasn't sure I wanted to tell them my story. I didn't trust them, and they didn't trust me either. I cried, because I felt there was no warmth there at all—just doors closing me out. I said, "I was in Vietnam, too. Maybe I didn't walk in the jungle with leeches on my legs or sleep on the ground in the mud, but I saw every part of the war you saw, and worse. I ache from it, and I want to talk about it, and I want some support, too."

They told me I should go over to the General Hospital and have a little talk with the intensive care unit nurses, who were the proper people for me to be speaking to. I said, "I don't think they have any idea what Vietnam was about." But the vet center thought that because those nurses had seen the same kind of injuries that I had seen, they would understand. Well, we may have seen similar medical problems, but in very different conditions! The vets didn't invite me back to join the group. The facilitator quit because of what had happened to me, and also because he felt the vets weren't growing. They didn't want to feel, and they knew that if I were in the group, there would be tears. They wanted to sit there and tell war stories. They didn't want to let go, and they sure didn't want to cry.

I did join another group with two other nurses, but it still wasn't what I needed. The facilitator wasn't sufficiently trained, and I felt some of the vets needed a lot more help than the group could give them. Some of them had really deep problems and were very angry, which scared me and the other women. They were wonderful people, but it was frightening how much anger they had, and how much sadness.

I think all Vietnam veterans who made it back said to them-selves over there, "I am not going to feel." If they felt too much, maybe they weren't going to get home. They'd go crazy or kill themselves or be killed. I think the people who felt most deeply did often get killed, trying to save a buddy, or they were unable to kill. I had a lot of feeling, being a nurse, but deep down I knew that I couldn't allow myself to feel very much or I would go crazy.

What's wrong with so many vets is they've never had the chance to grieve over the deaths and all the destruction they saw. Suddenly they're back home in a place where people don't care and don't listen. When I came back, nobody ever asked me anything but trivial questions about Vietnam. Maybe they thought I didn't want to talk about it, but they never asked. More than anything, I wanted to talk about it.

There is a time when you have to start letting go, a time when you have to put your energy back into life, into the present. I think there are a lot of veterans who don't want to let go of Vietnam, now that it's okay to be a Vietnam vet and angry. A lot of them don't want to get rid of that anger, and they're stuck. I don't ever want to lose my anger or sadness or feelings I have about Vietnam, but I don't want to go around being angry.

When I came back I kept in touch for a while with several good friends I made in Vietnam. But when I've had the chance to see them, I've made excuses not to. In fact, once I drove right through Jim's town. Part of me wanted to see them again, but another part of me couldn't stand to have the past brought back again. Of course, it comes back often enough in other ways: an episode of M.A.S.H. or nightmares. I think there's a part of me that will never stop being sad, for the rest of my life.

What I learned in Vietnam was how powerful and tragic our American wisdom was. It took many years before I had the courage to face my feelings but, when I finally did, I knew I had a special responsibility to tell people what we had seen and done there. I wanted to be a part of the conscience of America so I could help make sure another war would never happen. I belong to the Veterans' Speakers Alliance and we speak to high schools, community clubs, rally, and activist organizations. What's happening in Central America is most important to me now. I visited Nicara-

gua with other Vietnam vets, and after we returned we hoped that by sharing what we saw we could touch the hearts and minds of other Americans.

MARGARET KILGORE

Margaret Kilgore, a UPI correspondent, spent twenty months in Vietnam, reporting from Saigon and the DMZ, near Da Nang.

VIETNAM

The Tet Offensive of 1968 was underway, but most of the fellows who were covering Vietnam for UPI were coming home because their tours were over and UPI was running out of people to replace them. H.L. Stevenson, who is now managing editor of UPI in New York, was talking to some of the guys at a cocktail party at the Press Club, trying to interest them in going. I said, "How about me, coach?" and Stevenson said, "What's a nice girl like you want to go over there for?" I said, "I don't know, but I think I have a right to be considered!" So he said, "Write me a letter," which I did. It got filed away and I forgot about it.

One day, in November of 1969, Stevenson called me up and asked me to lunch, and he said, "Remember that letter you wrote in '68? Well, how would you like to go?" I said, "I'd love to!" I left for Vietnam in January, 1970. My tour was originally for eighteen months but I stayed for twenty-one because they were in the middle of the Laotian incursion and the Cambodian invasion and the start of the American pull-out, and the rigged "election" of President Thieu. I was too curious to leave before the end of the story!

I was very excited about going. I've always been very ambitious, and this was an opportunity to further my career. I was a little apprehensive, however, because although I had a lot of political background, I didn't have much background on the war. Despite all the briefings they give you, you still feel that you don't understand who is fighting whom and why. Unfortunately, the way it was in Vietnam, I never did find out why. It was scary going into

a situation I didn't understand, especially after all the awful stories I'd heard. Whereas I was a sophisticated Washington reporter, I had never worked overseas before or been in a war zone.

Saigon was terribly overgrown, having a population that had grown from three thousand to three million almost overnight. I saw a lot of hurt and maimed there, but then you could see that all over Asia. I was there to be a reporter and so I had to remain emotionally detached. I had to be objective about what I saw—except that you can't cover a war and not have some feeling about it. Sometimes it was very sad, especially seeing all those children without much of a future, or the educated people who had little hope of ever getting out or doing what they were educated to do.

But if you want to know the truth, I had a pretty good time at first, when I wasn't out on stories. I like men and I like to work with them. They gave me great respect and were very nice to me. I've always been professional in my work and they treated me professionally, and I think the three or four of us women who were over there would all agree we were treated well.

I did pretty much what I wanted to do there, even go to movie theaters which were liable to get blown up because, as my Vietnamese translator said to me once, "You should do every day what you want because maybe tomorrow you can't." That's a rather good way to live, I think. Besides, I found it more terrifying to sit in the bureau with rats crawling out of the sandbags and jumping over my feet. That was much more terrifying than the threat of maybe being blown up when I went out for dinner. We'd stand on the roof of the Caravel Hotel and watch the rockets falling. We got very used to the rocket attacks, hearing them and seeing them. People went about their business from day to day with the idea that if you got blown up you got blown up, and that was it, the luck of the draw.

I will always be very grateful to United Press for letting me go. I consider my time in Vietnam as the single most interesting thing I've ever done in my life. However, I never thought those two years were thrilling at all. It was hard to be there and hard to live there. We got tired of putting up with things, of having trouble getting even the simplest necessities.

I had a one room apartment in a hotel, with a hot plate. I became locally famous for my spaghetti dinners. Spaghetti,

because I could only boil things! I'll tell you about the most discouraging day of my life over there, and I know it must have been very discouraging because I think I'll never forget how awful it was. I got up at six o'clock in the morning to fly to Da Nang. We went in a military plane and were up there all day, coming back to Saigon at dusk. On the way I got my period, there in the middle of all those men. I was extremely uncomfortable and it wasn't made any easier by the fatigues I had to wear, which were very hot. Then, I was met at the hotel steps by a big rat. When I got up to my room and turned on the water, nothing came out but mud. The lights were out. Nothing worked. I thought, "I'm going home!" Lousy plumbing, lousy sewers, lousy lighting, nothing working. Americans are so efficient, and the Vietnamese never seemed to be very bothered when things didn't work. They'd just shrug and giggle.

Getting through an ordinary day was pretty challenging. I'd get up and turn on the Air Force Vietnam radio station, which was taped for the military, and take a shower with a hose that came out of the wall, get dressed, eat breakfast and go to the bureau. We'd talk over what had happened during the night and what assignments we had to cover that day, days that usually lasted twelve or fourteen hours. It was a funny way of life because if there wasn't some war action going on, it was incredibly dull. This was true all over the country. At least when you work for the wire service, though, there's always a lot of writing to do about what had gone on overnight, and that kept us busier.

We spent a lot of time covering Congressmen who were "seeing the war." Many were there just to criticize and some just to observe, but they were mostly a waste of time. I felt the same way the military felt about them—we just wanted to get on with the war and quit having to entertain politicians. They were a drag, but then they also brought us news from home. We never knew about fashion, for instance, whether the mini skirt was in or out, and sometimes they would keep us posted on things like that.

Now, I was essentially there as a political correspondent, not a combat correspondent, covering the U.S. Embassy and the Paris peace talks and the Thieu government; but, I did get around. Everybody went out because it was impossible to get an idea of the war by staying in Saigon. The reporters of the time were criticized

for covering the war from the bar of the Caravel Hotel, but that wasn't true. I believe there were twenty-three journalists who were killed or captured and never heard from again.

I would go up to the DMZ, near Da Nang, and cover what the hospitals were doing for the wounded. They did a marvelous job, just like our military did. Once I was in a helicopter, sitting in the back with a reporter from the *Christian Science Monitor,* and all of a sudden we noticed it was on fire. We landed and they dropped the back door and we ran, then watched the son-of-a-gun blow up. We drove back to Saigon!

Another time I was taken up to the DMZ in a helicopter and we had to get out because there was shooting nearby. The pilot didn't want to land because the ground was marshy and he might get stuck and not be able to take off. So we jumped out into what was a potential minefield, and we ran to the road and jumped on an armored personnel carrier that was there. I jumped but I missed the step and lost my balance and fell and broke my tailbone. That was my war injury.

I extended my stay for three months to cover the election. I was in the middle of the story and wanted to follow it through; and also, after two years, being there became a way of life. I'd been out of the United States so long I wasn't dying to get home. I wasn't dying to stay either, but I was used to being there. I think if I'd been offered a post that would've prolonged my tour, I would've stayed. However, I didn't feel bad about finally leaving. You go on to other things. You can't cover war all your life, particularly such an unglamorous war. A bunch of us in the bureau were leaving together. The American pull-out was starting, so a lot of the people I had been with were leaving too. I wasn't leaving friends behind, except for the Vietnamese who had worked for us at the bureau, many of whom I subsequently helped to get out. I felt I had done my time, but the experience of being over there, being permitted to cover the war, to travel all over the world, was a great thing! I wouldn't trade it. Besides, it will look so good in my obituary.

Margo St. James, a prostitute, numbered many veterans among her clients.

UNITED STATES

The military men I saw as a prostitute behaved in different ways depending on what rank they were and what war they'd been in. The guys who'd been in the mud in the foxholes in Vietnam came back to a country that hadn't supported the war and really didn't want the vets back. A lot of them had big drug problems. I saw many young vets in the Tenderloin strung out on heroin, taken care of by a junkie whore, in a kind of partnership.

In my experience, it's only these young vets who get violent. They fought an unpopular war, which World War II was not, and they were younger when they went into Vietnam than the others. They felt ostracized and discriminated against, even by the older vets. The easiest person to take angry feelings out on is a woman because she doesn't have power. A hooker has no power at all, no public voice at all to complain with. She wouldn't be believed even if she were listened to.

I was luckier than some. The only time I had a violent experience with a vet was with a little Marine who tried to choke me. It was late and I was sleepy and everyone else in the house was asleep, and by the time I realized he was trying to choke me I couldn't say a word or cry for help. I guess he could've killed me. That happens. But I pretended that I didn't know he was attacking me. I just flipped him over on his back and said, "I'll get on top for awhile," and hurried him up and got him out of there. He never said a word.

I think it's dangerous to deprive men of touching and relationships of any kind. Especially these young men who have had a great lack of sex education to begin with, and who've been trained

to be killers. In cities like Colorado Springs, where they cracked down on whores and ran them out of town, they realized they had to have hookers to keep the lid on. As soon as the whores were all run out of town there wasn't anyplace for these guys to go and kibitz and nobody to fuck over, and so they turned on the town girls, who were getting raped at a much higher rate than before.

Men who come back from war, who are or have been under stress, are especially in need of comfort from women. When they come back from Europe or Vietnam they can't find that comfort because our culture is more uptight, with lots of people trying to get in the way of men and women getting together for carnal comfort, especially commercial carnal comfort.

A prostitute gives a man a place to feel safe, where he doesn't have to fear rejection. Men tell prostitutes things they wouldn't tell anybody else. It's like talking to a stranger on a bus, someone you aren't ever going to see again.

I think the government should be paying hookers for taking care of veterans nobody else wants to have anything else to do with. If our work were legitimized, then these men, vets or not, could have a chance for intimate relationships. The feeling of closeness is important to handicapped vets especially, the feeling of being with someone who isn't repulsed by them if they've lost limbs or have been scarred in a war.

These vets were always very appreciative for what I did for them. I met with very little violence, but I did see a lot of bitterness. If some guy was into denial, you'd get a lot of anger dumped on you. For instance, if a guy is paralyzed and he thinks he's going to walk again, there's a rage bubbling under the surface because he's not walking yet and he feels he could be.

When a man suffers the loss of a limb, or some other part of his body, he really needs sex with somebody to feel reaffirmed and whole. It's a heavy trip, because the guy really does appreciate a hooker a lot and can fall in love really fast. So it's hard working with people like this. You hold them and act affectionate and responsive to them, and they need that. They're very lonely. Everybody's turned off in the street. They don't dare catch anyone's eye in a subway or look at anyone on a bus. There's tremendous loneliness—this was especially true for the Vietnam vet—and the

prohibition of commercial sex only increases this sense of loneliness and rejection.

These men don't fear rejection from a prostitute, though. They might if they thought she was a sweet young girl who had never seen mutilation before. Then they might have some inhibition to overcome. But usually people don't expect to be rejected by a prostitute. They feel she's an outlaw, a pariah, one of the downtrodden. Besides, men consider a whore to be a public woman. They expect service, on their terms, and don't expect such service to be refused.

I talked a lot to the handicapped vets. Most of them were more like regular tricks, maybe more militaristic. But with those who were more screwed up I'd spend maybe eighty percent of the hour talking to them. Sex was incidental. Sometimes they liked talking to me so much they didn't want to take up the hour doing anything else.

These guys never worried about what they said to me. They didn't feel upset or found out or betrayed, having a hooker knowing things about them. They felt support from me. If they could get out the real painful things, they'd be rid of them.

Later on, I felt I was probably one of the very few women they would ever see in such a very intimate way, and I felt good about that. I took a professional pride, so to speak, in helping these guys cope. It would've taken a psychiatrist a hell of a lot longer, because a psychiatrist just sits there without getting down to it. I found I could get to what their problem was in just a few minutes; almost instant communication. And trust. That is what was really instant, because their money buys the trust. They don't have to worry about your angle because they know your angle is simply money. I mean, with psychiatrists it's money too, but they're pretending it's something else.

I had one trick who was a police officer, sent to Cambodia in 1963 as an advisor to train their police. He wasn't physically injured but he had changed psychically. He had been kind of a macho guy, but nice. He disappeared for a few years, and I'd write him letters and he would never reply. Of course they were all antiwar letters, so maybe that's why I never heard from him. Then he came back and we met again. He had got to where he had no

sense of the worth of human life. Women and children were nothing to him. He'd talk about these twelve-year-old girls who were "so lovely." I thought, "My God, he was never into pederasty before." But over there in that war atmosphere anything goes and the poverty is great and people would sell their little girls to pimps who would sell them to the officers and their staff.

I thought that was truly disgusting. For a long time, I couldn't even bear to talk to him. The worst part was, he didn't even seem to see anything wrong with it. Before the war he'd been kind and considerate; it was a bad thing that happened to this guy.

Ironically, what men need, in such an anti-life enterprise as war, is the pro-life qualities of warmth, comfort and sex. That's why the Army encourages camp followers and always has. However, that causes problems that come home to roost! They won't tell you that penicillin was used prophylactically in Vietnam, that the boys were shot up before they went out to screw around, but that's caused a real problem here because that practice has resulted in a strain of penicillin-resistant gonorrhea which is epidemic in several cities. We're not checking these guys out, or quarantining them; we just let them right back into the country to infect the women here, and people still continue to blame VD on whores.

Anyway, the roles I found myself playing mostly with all these vets, who were away from home and lonely, were that of earth-mother or sister. It mattered that I was there for them, and even after fifteen years there are men I stay in contact with, although I don't see them sexually anymore. They come over and see me when they need help and keep track of me. I have quite a fan club, actually. They give me testimonials all the time: "She changed my life;" "She kept me from being a gambler"; "She saved me from being an alcoholic."

The "whore with a heart of gold" is really a myth. Most whores are mean and sentimental and don't have a heart of gold at all. Now, I have a mean streak and a sharp tongue, but I guess in ways I kind of fit the stereotype in that I'm nurturing, like my mother was. When you're older you can accept more. I've become more of a diplomat now, and though I'm very outspoken, I try to say things in a way that won't seem offensive. I never tried to be inoffensive when I was younger. I thought that was kind of sissy.

I know I did some good, in spite of my toughness, because without intimacy and without acceptance, men like those vets don't have hope; and they can't make anything of their lives until they have a glimmer of hope. They can then move on to have a relationship or start a business or say, "To heck with it, I'll go to hookers all my life!" If they don't have enough money or attractiveness to find someone to marry, then they have to buy sex and intimacy. They have to have it, because intimacy is something we must have to live. We all need to be comforted in this world, especially the downtrodden and the forgotten and the guys who have nothing the world wants.

KATHY KANE

Kathy Kane was a flight attendant on military flights carrying infantry to and from Vietnam.

VIETNAM

I was a professional singer and bass player in a rock band, but when the group fell apart and I couldn't seem to find another job, I interviewed with Saturn Airlines, a charter line, and a week later they called me to come to airline school. I really liked it, but I didn't realize in training that I was to be flying to Vietnam.

I went into stewardessing because of the glamour of the job. I had visions of myself flying to the Caribbean and to Europe, and it wasn't until towards the end of training that they started telling us we were going to be flying the military and that they had to be handled differently than tourist passengers, that they were used to following orders and we couldn't assume that they would do anything in an emergency but just stay in their seats until we told them to get out. They were like sheep.

Even then I didn't realize we would be flying into Vietnam. I thought we'd be flying officers around, or military families, and not until the very last were we informed we'd be flying soldiers. I was oblivious to all the suffering going on, and I was really excited to go.

At the beginning I was a little nervous about doing my job right, but not about going to Vietnam. At that time, unless you were in college and had a social consciousness, war was just a game going on far away in Southeast Asia. It wasn't real. I went with a lot of trust that we would never be put in any kind of dangerous situation, but the reality was that it was very dangerous. Although I never heard of a passenger jet being shot down in Vietnam, when we were shot at we often got bullet holes in our wings.

When we came into Vietnam we'd fly at a very high altitude

and then just before we were going to land we'd divebomb to the strip. Ben Wa, near Saigon, is where we landed the most. They had a rule that we couldn't fly into Vietnam between eleven o'clock at night and four o'clock in the morning because that's the time the heavy rocketing occurred, but it seems we were never on time and that's exactly when we'd arrive.

If there was heavy shelling when we were there, they wouldn't let us take off. They'd give us flak jackets and then walk us over to the bunkers which were little caves made of sandbags. We thought it was kind of a fun adventure, but the military guys escorting us were very serious. They'd say, "Listen, ladies, we're glad you're not scared to death. On the other hand, we wish you would take this more seriously."

I remember all of us stews feeling a sense of responsibility to be good to the men, even women who wouldn't have ordinarily spoken to passengers on a regular tourist flight.

When you got into the front of the plane and looked down, it was like a long cattle car full of guys, all with their hair shaved off, just like carbon copies of each other. I was twenty-one when I started and twenty-three when I stopped, but these guys were all seventeen and eighteen years old, and they seemed so young. They were all very scared and very quiet. There was no partying or talking.

We would generate conversation with them in the beginning, but after a few months it became difficult and painful. I began to realize what these boys were going to experience. We flew only infantry and that's where the high casualty rates were. They all knew that statistically one out of every three of them was not going to return home, and there they'd sit in those rows of three, knowing just two of them would make it.

I can't say which was worse, going over with the guys who didn't know what they were facing, or coming back with the guys who knew only too well. The hard part about going over was that I knew it would probably be ten times worse for them than they ever thought it was going to be. It made me feel guilty that I had a better idea of the horrors they were going to face than they did. They had been purposefully improperly prepared for what they were going to face, but then if they had been properly prepared there would've been a lot more AWOLs than there were. I felt sure

they had been trained in World War II tactics, and weren't prepared for the kind of guerrilla warfare they would be fighting.

One of the things they'd tell us about was how they had to go around killing civilians, women and children, to protect themselves. They didn't know they would have to do that. When their friends were killed by Vietnamese who looked innocent, they realized they could trust nobody in that country, including the whores even the most naive guys ended up with.

It was like day and night between the boys we took over and the ones we brought home. I felt I took over babies and brought back cynical old men. I remember once we were in Camranh Bay. It was the very first time I'd gotten off the plane and gone into the terminal. The guys waiting to get on our plane were lying all over the floor, sleeping on their duffle bags with their rifles in their arms. Suddenly I realized they were just about to give up their guns for the first time in at least a year. They'd get on the plane, and the center of the blue carpet would be all red from what they tracked in on their boots. I now believe it was Agent Orange. The jungle was wiped out by this stuff for maybe a mile around, and all the land around the airports was red because it had been sprayed with a defoliant so that snipers couldn't hide there and shoot at the planes.

They went over to Vietnam in perfect uniforms, but when we saw them again, they wore big saber-tooth necklaces or headbands and much longer hair. They were all tan and looked quite a bit older. A lot of them were into drugs and they'd talk about them a lot—marijuana was the most popular, but they were also into heroin and opium. It got so bad towards the end, that the military would bring dogs on the planes. Usually all they would do was confiscate the drugs, but you should have seen the panic when those dogs were brought on board.

A lot of the guys had jungle rot all over their hands, arms, and feet. Many wore brass bracelets which were notched for every person they'd killed, and they were really proud of them, the more notches the better. Some of the guys would show us pictures of themselves holding up Vietnamese heads they'd just cut off. Even though I was really repelled by some of their stories, I don't ever remember judging the guys for them. I felt they were just as much victims as the people they'd killed. Most of them were country

boys who had never even heard of the peace movement—that's how naive and dumb they were when they went over there.

Most of them were very bitter, but were happy to be getting home. They did not want to stay in the army, feeling like they had wasted a year of their lives, but wanted to get home and forget about it as soon as possible. A lot of them had really sad stories about girlfriends back home who had broken up with them while they were gone.

It was actually the quiet ones I was most scared of. You could just feel a kind of seething inside them. Some of them wanted to go back again. They had learned to live like animals and you could picture them becoming mercenaries, which some of them did.

We learned not to wake up a man who was asleep. He would come out of sleep fighting, just flailing. We'd try to get the guy sitting next to him to wake him up, but they usually wouldn't do it. Sometimes a girl might get upset with one of the weird guys, but I never felt that way. I had a lot of empathy for them. Fear, also, but I found myself often talking to them because no one else on the plane would. It hurt to listen to them; they were just walking bundles of pain, and you could feel it.

Even so, I know that everything I've heard and read and seen is just a drop in the bucket about what really happened to people in Vietnam. I believe it was one of the ugliest experiences anyone could ever have on this earth. It was a terrible war in an area of complete corruption where people were so desperate they'd do anything for money. Our guys had no power on some levels and incredible power on others, particularly when it came to women. When people are feeling powerless, and they are suddenly in a position of power, they are apt to use it in destructive ways. I know the men gave us respect they did not give the Vietnamese women, which always bothered me. Racial prejudice was rampant then.

On the flights over, we were mother or big sister images for the men, but on the way back it was clear that we could never have any possible idea what they'd experienced, and they were very cynical and angry about it. Sometimes I felt they were angry with us because we were still kind of soft and laughing, and I got the feeling they thought we were shallow, which was probably true. It

seemed to me that would become an inevitability in all their relationships from then on with anybody who hadn't been in Vietnam.

When I was back in the States waiting for my next flight, people would ask me why I was doing these flights, and there was a strong implication that I was supporting the war by taking troops over there. I'd explain to people that at least I was sensitive to and could understand something of what the men were experiencing and what they were feeling. I knew I was taking many of them over there to die, but I didn't feel responsible for that. I felt it was good for me to be there for them, to listen and comfort them. I didn't realize it at the time, but what I was giving them was love. I wanted them to have as much of a pleasant experience going over there as possible, because I felt that maybe it would give them a good memory and hope. I really believe that if you have hope you have a better chance to survive.

As time went on, seeing all this, I got more and more antiwar until finally I was travelling around with big peace signs all over my suitcase. A lot of the girls became radically antiwar. I think most of us started out pretty oblivious, but what we saw changed us all.

I listen to Reagan, and people like him talk about war, and I wonder now, "Do they really understand the price?" I don't think they do. And to have expected so much from these vets, to expect them to come home and get a job and carry on as usual—they don't have the personal resources to do that. They were so young when Vietnam happened to them, with so little life experience before it.

I have to admit I do feel some guilt being involved in what now seems to me to be a kind of conspiracy, even though I did it unwittingly and even if I can justify it by saying I made the trip easier for the men. I am antiwar now, and I think I could've done something else, like demonstrating here at home. But, if we ever get close to being in another war, I'll be the first one with a picket sign.

HELEN ADAMS

*Helen Adams, an antiwar activist, was part of an under-
ground railroad for draft resisters and deserters during the
Vietnam War.*

UNITED STATES

When I was nineteen, I took my newborn son to the well-baby
clinic in the lower east side of Manhattan where I was living and
where I was a student at City College. I had this beautiful little
baby boy and the woman aide at the clinic was telling me about
booster injections, and she said, "You do this series of injections,
and then after he's eighteen the army will take him over and
they'll take care of it."

I remember ripping my baby out of her arms! "Cannon
Fodder" came into my mind, that I was raising my child to be
shipped out as fodder for the war machine. At that moment I felt,
'You'll never get my son!" That experience seemed to imprint
something in me.

The Vietnam War came up when my son was around five years
old. My reactions to the war, like those of other college students,
were feelings of excitement. It was like "break down the
Machine!" There was an enormous amount of comradeship and
solidarity in the resistance movement that was emerging in New
York. We really felt, in our innocence, that we could stop the war!

I was absolutely swept away by the emotion of the times. Defin-
ing my identity and working together with other people in this
cause made the Sixties one of the most moving times in my life. It
was my first experience of a community outside the narrow con-
fines of a family, so it had a kind of spiritual aspect to it, something bigger than myself.

We ran a lot of risks. I went to work for the Bread and Puppet
Theatre, which was the artistic wing of the war resistance move-

ment. We did neighborhood plays, organizing for draft resistance and other political issues. My son was in the plays too. That was my livelihood for maybe two or three years.

The first play I did with them was a small mask and mime piece called "Fire," dedicated to the war resisters who had immolated themselves in protest to Vietnam. That was very moving, and it made me feel that it was not only a deep commitment to those deaths, but to life, as well. Part of the draw was the challenge of being able to change the thinking of the country and try to establish a new order of democratic thinking, but it was also a lot of fun.

The establishment soon became aware of the position we had taken and the police in New York were alerted to stop our plays, to stop any kind of street organizing. Within a matter of a few months the whole wonderful experience began to close down, and it began to move toward violence. What had been a way of going into a neighborhood with a street play to express a political point of view became more and more difficult to do. Activists were hassled in any kind of public situation; we couldn't get licenses to gather; or, when we had a meeting, it was disrupted.

In reaction, our side became polarized too. It was extremely distressing to realize that what had been an enthusiastic idea for social change, once under pressure, became a violent situation.

I continued to take a pacifist stand, so I lost my position not only in the eyes of the establishment as a resister, but in my own group. Those of us who were pacifists were alienated from those who were going to go underground in what was later to become the Weather Underground. We had nowhere to go. There was no way we could continue, even in our own eyes, with what now seemed like silly, childlike tactics. It became a crisis for me, and I stayed with the group longer than I probably should have.

By 1968, there were street confrontations, many beatings. The police were singling out people and hassling them, sometimes beating them in order to stop the organizing against the war. In the antiwar march to Washington, the group I was with was cut off not by the police but by people who objected to the march proceeding; conservatives, just regular old American people. We were cornered and the men were badly beaten and I got two cracked ribs.

It became progressively more confrontational, almost as if you had to go to war to stop the war. That was not acceptable to me. I lost a lot of friends over the use of guns. I felt they were a bunch of intellectuals who had never seen the sight of blood and had no real sense of what this violence was really about.

That's why I decided to join the part of the underground that was committed to pacifist resistance. Young men in the movement who refused the draft and took jail sentences, ranging from two to five years, needed support, advice, and connection with other people. Many others were taking a position alone in various parts of the country, so a loose network was set up for informational exchanges at army posts or in towns connected to them, and draft counseling was made available for people who wanted to leave the country after being drafted.

My job was to assist these young men, some of them deserters, some resisters. Of course the whole thing was illegal, and I was not always in agreement with the position a refuser or a deserter might take. But to my mind, anybody that resisted the draft was somebody I should help. I took that position even though individuals upset me, because of their own lack of courage. However, one form of refusal is to run away. On the other hand, there were some of the most extraordinary souls I ever met, young men who were able to take a position of conscience and with complete clarity go through with it! I certainly respected them.

I obtained false documents to get several young men out of the country by secret means. They had to be moved from city to city, be fed, housed, and gotten through. That was my job, essentially, as part of an underground railroad that proceeded by a series of safe houses and sympathetic people who were able to obtain papers. You made your telephone calls from public telephones, and you didn't let it get too close to home. This was the work I was doing and I would do it again. I felt it was an act of honor to refuse the bloodshed of an unjust war.

The pressures on my son were enormous because of the stand I took. In our house there were always people who were fearful of being apprehended, and he was aware, too, of my organizing activities—choosing the guard detail or my having to go out and use public phones. In a way it made him very protective toward me. I think that some of his stand against violence now is because

of my ideals. I wish I could rid myself of that feeling and believe that he had taken his stand on his own. On the other hand, society was happy to hypnotize him in one direction, he might as well have a contrapuntal piece of hypnosis from me!

I also think he felt a certain protectiveness toward the underdog, as do so many resisters, which I don't like. We did not feel powerful. There was never a moment when we really thought, unless we had a mammoth collective event, that we were going to change anything. There's a certain kind of energy that you have when you're up against the wall. It's like "do or die." It's exciting! But it keeps you an underdog and you are never in a position to direct things as you would have them be. You are always in negative reaction to somebody else's direction; "Not that, not that ... " For me, having authority is not appealing, unless it's in my narrow area of expertise, and then I would like someone else to have authority in their area. In that way we can be collective. But the way the human mind is set up, our tendency is to see ourselves either above or below rather than equal and different. But this was the vision I had. To have authority in the establishment's viewpoint means to have the power in *all* categories. I don't like that.

My present husband was badly maced. He still has bad scarring in his lungs, and he was beaten so that he had to have brain surgery. When I met him he was still carrying his scars with him, and the scars were also in his emotions. He was a very bitter person. I could see that with both of us meeting with that point of view we could easily have gotten involved in embittered political groups. But something in us reacted to the joy and spontaneity of life.

I had dropped out of graduate school, which had made my dependency on the movement even more important. I had cut myself off entirely. It took me years to go back to finish my degree. For a long time I felt I would be committed to radical politics the rest of my life, that I would go from one organizing job to another. Then when the movement started to lose its intensity, I realized I ought to be back on my own. That was a terrible dark night of the soul, a night of soul searching. It felt as if everything had dissolved: my point of view, my group, everything. However, by then I'd met my second husband, my son was growing up, and I could see the possibility of at least making a family.

89

Those years in the movement: it's a heightened life, and you never realize how exciting life is until you don't have that kind of life anymore. If anything had that energy in it now, I'd be the first one on the front line!

*Marian Shelton was a director of the National League of
Families, which pursues information about POWs and
MIAs; her husband was shot down on an illegal bombing
mission over Laos in 1965.*

LAOS

Charles and I were married as soon as I got out of high school,
when I was seventeen. I had my first baby right away and ended
up having four children in less than five years. Charles joined the
ROTC, and in his final year of college he was told to sign up for
flight training. He called me and asked how I felt about it. I said,
"It's your life, do what you want," and he said, "Just tell me yes
or no." I said, "Well, then, no." And he said, "I've already signed
up."

After flight training he got sent to Germany, but since our kids
were having health problems, I couldn't follow him for six
months. I made the trip with three children and I was seven
months pregnant with the fourth. It was an absolute nightmare.

Finally he was sent to Vietnam in 1962 as a reconnaissance advisor. He was over there ten months, and I moved back to Louis-
ville, Kentucky, to wait until he came home. The military said
then that I couldn't tell anyone Charles was in Vietnam, so I
couldn't even tell my kids, who were really curious. I guess our
men weren't supposed to be over there.

Charles came home at Christmas. He walked into the house and
said, "This is a nice house you have here," just like he was a
stranger. He seemed different. I had to get used to him being
around again. I hadn't seen this man in almost a year, and
because he's my husband he's supposed to move right in and sleep
with me again and be in charge of things.

Finally, Charles got orders for Okinawa, and I followed him a

91

month later with the five children I had by that time. My husband was a very jealous man, and he always said he liked me barefoot and pregnant, which I was mostly.

He left Okinawa for Thailand the day after Easter Sunday, 1965. He was supposed to be there for thirty days, flying on sorties into Laos and Vietnam. I had been invited one evening to dinner at the squadron commander's home. When I got there, the commander came in and said, "I've got some good news and some bad news. The bad news is your husband's plane was shot down today; the good news is he's on the ground and okay. We've got to get him out, and I'll call you by midnight to let you know if we have." I remember sitting there crying. I should have told the children myself, but I couldn't. The commander told me he'd tell them, and I let him. That was one of the worst things I've ever done.

They called me back at midnight and told me he was on the other side of the fence, but that I was to stay in Okinawa because they might still be able to rescue him. I stayed until June, and then took the children home. I thought I might as well wait for him there. They made several rescue attempts over the years, but I've always felt they'd get him out. I still do.

When I got back to the States I bought a car and drove all over the country trying to find a place to live. It was awful to be put back in a civilian community, knowing no one. I couldn't even tell anyone about my husband being shot down over Laos because we weren't supposed to be flying over Laos in those days.

I remember my mother pacing the floor at night, sobbing and praying because my brother was missing in action in World War II. He was declared an MIA but nobody ever knew what became of him. I often think how hard this situation is on mothers. This may be a terrible thing to say, but you can replace a husband. You can't replace a son. Now, I'll never have a husband again like Charles, and I've never remarried, but to know a son from the time he was a baby and then to lose him would hurt terribly. A child is part of you, a husband isn't.

Charles escaped numerous times, and I was told he was kept in shackles in a cave because of that. He supposedly turned a desk over on three North Vietnamese soldiers and then killed them with his bare hands. He was considered incorrigible.

Not long after, I heard he had been put in a shallow ditch with bars on top of it and a guard had to stand by with a hand grenade to keep Charles from escaping. Oh, it hurt me to hear all these things! He was such a sweetheart and we'd been together fourteen years. He was my first and only love, and to think of them doing all that to him ... . Finally I just couldn't think about it.

I'm trying to face the possibility that my husband has died, because to have been living in conditions like that for over twenty years is horrible. In my heart I hope that he got killed, not starved to death or tortured for all this time. And yet I know that no matter what, he would rather be alive.

The POW cases are reviewed, and the military decides whether or not your husband should be declared dead. They tried to declare my husband dead in 1972, and I've fought them ever since. It would be devastating if they did declare Charles dead, because it would be like they'd given up on him, or they didn't care.

In 1973, Viva, the people who made the POW bracelets, asked me to go to Southeast Asia on a fact-finding mission. I didn't think we'd find any prisoners, or that by some miracle I'd see Charles on some street. But I thought somehow I might be able to find out something.

We met the Vietnamese and the Viet Cong in Saigon. We showed them photographs, but they denied having seen the men in them. It was scary over there because we were watched the whole time. Our telephone lines were tapped and our rooms were bugged. One time I was standing by the window of my room, thinking about Charles and my children, and softly crying to myself. The landlady came to ask me if I was okay, that the floor-boy had said my eyes were sad. But, I hadn't been out at all that day. That's how keenly our rooms were bugged.

Later that year, 1973, the National League of Families asked me to run for the board, and I became its director for 1973-1974. We wives of MIAs found we could make some changes and make the government pay some attention to us.

One night I was watching a television special on "Nightline" about the trip of some League members to Laos. They showed pictures of the inside of the Pathet Lao cave where Charles had been held, and at one point the Laotian guide said, "At one time

there were two pilots kept in here." And one of the League members asked if one of them was Charles. The Laotian said the name sounded familiar, and then he said, "They died, and they were buried here." He pointed to a muddy hole. Then he said that a bomb had landed on the grave and had obliterated the bodies. I knew it was hardly possible, but still I was stunned to be sitting there in my living room looking at what they were saying was my husband's grave.

I heard about Charles for years, from the Freedom of Information Act files, from the CIA and the Air Force, and other agencies. I also heard from a pilot in 1967, who had just gotten back from Vietnam, that he knew Charles had been shipped north.

Through it all, I've always believed he would come home, but I'm not as optimistic as I once was. I think I lost some hope when the POWs came home and Charles didn't come home with them. We stood by the phone for twenty-four hours when the Vietnamese gave out a list of those who were coming home. The Air Force called to tell me his name was not on the list, but then Laos never sent a list.

I really feel that we can't allow our government to give up on them. Even if my husband is dead, there still is somebody's husband or son over there. My husband is one of the strongest cases that prisoners are still alive over there, and I can't have him declared dead like all the other POWs have been, because then they might give up on them altogether, and that wouldn't be right.

I have worked continuously through the years on the prisoner-of-war issue. All I have learned has convinced me that there are still hundreds of live prisoners of war in Southeast Asia. There was a sighting of my husband in April, 1985, so chances are he's still alive now. He isn't the only one, though he is now considered the last POW in Indochina. President Reagan is directly responsible for keeping my husband in this status and not allowing him to be "given up" as an MIA. The Secretary of the Air Force told me the decision came straight down from the Administration.

I suspect the government is aware there are prisoners of war alive over there. Certain people in the Pentagon and in the State Department have been involved in this issue since the beginning. I could name names, but I won't. Because they were lazy or ineffec-

tive in the beginning, or ashamed that they've left these men over there, perhaps they want the issue to die. Maybe it's a cover-up for other activities, I don't know. It could be a combination of both. Kissinger never signed an agreement with Laos to get our men back, so we didn't. The only men we did get back were the ones who were taken from Laos right into North Vietnam.

When I was in Vietnam and Laos in 1973, I met with a delegation of North Vietnamese. I was seeking any information I could find regarding the fate of our POWs. When I asked specifically about my husband, I was told, "Why are you asking us when your own government says that they are all dead?"

Major Mark Smith and Sergeant Melvin McIntyre have brought a lawsuit against the government, and they are joined by Colonel Howard, winner of the Medal of Honor and once Smith and McIntyre's boss.

They are doing this because, in May of 1984, they were told by "a source" in Laos that if they waited on their side of the border, in Thailand, three prisoners of war would be brought out to them. But the POWs were to be brought out only to Smith and McIntyre. When this was reported, the two men were immediately taken off duty and sent back to Korea, and then sent home six months early. They have all the information—photographs and fingerprints and so on—but nobody will believe them. When Mark Smith told his general, the general said to him, "This is too hot for me to handle. The best thing for you to do if you ever want to make lieutenant colonel is to shred the evidence."

After much thought and soul-searching I have become a plaintiff in the suit, in the hope of compelling the President to bring our prisoners home. I think that if we can go to court and present all the information we have, then maybe we can see that he gets wind of what's going on so he˙ can do something about it.

We're suing the President, the Vice President, the Secretary of State, the Secretary of Defense, the Director of the Defense Intelligence Agency, and all of his predecessors. After we launched the suit, the government asked us to dismiss the case, but the judge wouldn't do it, though he did take Smith and McIntyre off the case as plaintiffs because they have no family members involved.

Look, I'm proud to be an American and enjoy the freedom we all take so much for granted. But those men who fought so

bravely for our country deserve their freedom too. For as long as one American remains a prisoner, not one of us is free.

Our military men know when they sign up that they might get captured, but they also believe that if this happens they will be rescued by their country, not abandoned. If we're really willing to leave this many of our men behind, then I believe our military will go to Hell. When a man goes to fight for his country, he's got to feel his country is willing to fight for him, too.

Chances are my husband is alive today. I wonder what he thinks about, what he knows. He was shot down before a man walked on the moon. He has a grandson he doesn't know about, whose birthday this year, incidentally, was on National POW and MIA Day. It was the only POW's only grandchild's birthday. Think of that.

RUTH SMITH

Ruth Smith, born in Mississippi, joined the Air Force for the opportunities it offered blacks; she never stopped fighting racial prejudice the twenty years she served.

UNITED STATES

I lived in Montgomery, Alabama, and at that time in the South there were few jobs for blacks, except as maids or nurses or teachers. Blacks couldn't work in offices or banks. I wanted to be a C.P.A., but that was out. This was in the fifties, a few years before Martin Luther King, Jr., and things were tough.

I went to college for two years, but didn't have the money to finish. I was determined, however, to get away. I had wanted to be in the Air Force ever since I was little. Basic training was tough, but I enjoyed it. We had to take tests to see what skills we had, and they were surprised I had good math skills. I was the only black woman in the math classes, and I could tell the teachers doubted my abilities.

After basic, I went "Permanent Party," and started to work in data processing, where I stayed. I wanted to be an officer, but my technical advisor suggested I wait and not go to officers' training school. I don't know why. It should have bothered me, but it didn't. I was young. Later I just gave up the idea.

I don't know if people segregate themselves, but in the South even in the Army blacks and whites tended to use separate facilities. Certain bathrooms were for blacks and others were for whites. One day a black woman came up to me when I was about to go in a cafeteria and she told me I should go to another one, farther away, that was used by "us." I told her I wouldn't allow myself to be segregated, that it was one Air Force and we were all equal in it. I went on in and sat with the whites, and it was okay. We had to have a law passed to integrate the military, and I was deter-

mined never to let myself be segregated by anyone in any way.

I spent three weeks in Wiesbaden where I had a wonderful time. I felt welcomed and was very proud to be an American in uniform in Germany. When I returned home I'd walk around very proud; I'd always wear my uniform and enjoyed it when people stared at me. There had been a stigma attached to going into the military at that time; a man I was dating told me only "bad girls" went into the service. I told him goodbye.

The end came when I was in a car wreck and hospitalized for sixteen months. At first I thought they would let me stay, but they wouldn't. I was devastated. I loved being in the military, and most of my experiences were good ones.

I got a job as a civilian doing data processing at the Presidio Army base. I had to quit, though, when they promoted another girl over me. I had more experience, more education, and I was the boss over the girl who was promoted. But she was white.

I knew it was racial prejudice, though that's something I don't like to talk about. It had happened before, when I was still in the service. A white man was promoted ahead of me, though I outranked him and was his boss. I had been recommended, too, but when the promotion was announced, I didn't get it.

When I was told, I went to the chaplain and cried. The second time it happened, at the Presidio, I didn't cry. I just walked into the head office and said, "If you're going to promote someone with less rank ahead of me, then I quit." I walked out and the next day I came in and cleaned out my desk and left. I wasn't going to put up with that kind of insult; I just couldn't face working there anymore. It hurts when you've done your job the best you can and that doesn't seem to matter.

I met my husband right here at Hamilton Air Force Base. We were married twenty-two years ago. My husband never went to war; he had a desk job. My son, who was my only child, was eighteen when he joined the military. It's hard for me to talk about him. It's a feeling that's indescribable to me.

He went to college, but he was very restless. He couldn't stand not having money in his pocket. Like all boys his age, he wanted a car and whatever goes with it; but, he couldn't have those things and go to college, too, so he enlisted in the Marines. I would've

preferred him going into the Air Force, but it was his choice to make. He joined for his country, too, because we were over there in Vietnam at that time and he felt we had to win. I felt that way, too, but now I think it cost too many lives in what amounted to a scrimmage. Sometimes I think that if we had just gotten him that car maybe he'd still be alive.

He was looking forward to coming home. He was due back in less than a month. He never wrote much about the war in his letters, and wasn't critical about what was going on. I guess he was just an obedient soldier. Later, guys over there started protesting the war, but in 1967, they were still doing what they were told.

I never saw him again. One day I got home from work and walked into the bedroom. The bed was turned back; my husband was acting strangely. But, before I could ask him what was going on, the doorbell rang. When I saw the chaplain from the base and another member of the Marine Corps, I knew why they were there. They said they came by to tell me what they had told my husband earlier, but had asked him not to tell me because they wanted to tell me themselves. They wanted to come before the telegram, which arrived an hour later.

A couple of years later, when everything was over and all the troops were being brought back from Vietnam, I was thinking that somehow maybe he was coming home too. I remember a Saturday afternoon, when my husband was away, a plane was supposed to land at Travis Air Force Base bringing the rest of the soldiers back. I called my husband and said, "Please come home; I need you right now." I was thinking maybe Larry would be on the plane. Of course my husband had seen him at the mortuary, but I couldn't accept it. Part of me knew that, but I kept thinking somehow there had been a mistake.

To this day I have thoughts of him. Not as often as before, when every day of my life I thought of Larry. I couldn't live like that. Then I blamed my husband for all the problems that made Larry enlist. We'd say to each other, "Maybe if you had been nicer, if I had been nicer, he wouldn't have gone." He didn't have to go; he volunteered. I guess he wanted to get away from home just like I did.

I'm not antiwar, being military myself and having so many rela-

tives in the military, but I became angry. When you lose your only son, it doesn't matter if it's Vietnam or World War II or Korea. Nothing lessens the pain.

Sometime later, my husband and I decided to settle down and buy a house. There were quite a few instances when we knew we couldn't buy or rent a house because we are black. I got bitter about not having this freedom, especially because my son had given his life for this country.

After my son was killed, there was nothing I could do about it except write a lot of letters. It helped. When that same year my husband got orders to go to Vietnam, I said, "Wait, you're not going to do this to me." I wrote to the President, and said, "We just lost our son, and you want my husband to go too?" Orders came down from the President, "Don't send Sergeant Smith to Vietnam." I was very relieved. My husband was too, but he really didn't want me to interfere.

I kept on writing letters. I wrote to other mothers and wives whose names appeared in the newspapers because they'd lost a son or a husband. It helped me to send them my condolences and tell them what had happened to me. I think the worst kind of pain there is in the world is when you lose a child. I've lost my father and I've lost other relatives, but when I lost my son it seemed like my life was ended. I couldn't see myself getting over it, being whole again, and I knew I wasn't alone in that feeling. I knew other mothers felt the same.

When my son was alive, I was still interested in my military career and wasn't interested in settling down and being a home-maker. When Larry was killed, it felt like my life was ending. We hadn't thought of adopting before, but I realized then that there were lots of kids who needed parents, and they could do something for my life and I could do something for their lives. That was true, and it helped very much. It seems like they're natural children, and they did help us make it through the pain with less bitterness.

Now I feel that if there's another war my adopted son won't go. He will not volunteer. I'll make sure he gets a deferment, and if he doesn't, I'll go with him to Canada. I'd prefer to do it through legal channels, though. That's my way—to write to the President, "This is my son you're taking. He's the only one I have left."

BETTY BETHARDS

Betty Bethards, wife of an American air force pilot, lost her son to "friendly fire" in Vietnam.

UNITED STATES

It is possible to get thoroughly brainwashed by all the crap the military tells you. When I married my first husband, an Air Force pilot, I had to go to an officers' wives briefing, and what they very clearly did was try to brainwash us. You're not supposed to tell your husband any problems you have at home; you're supposed to handle the children and all the little details of life because he's the one flying the bomber out there someplace. A military wife is supposed to struggle along by herself so that her husband won't have to think about those little unimportant things. The men were always on alert and their wives were often left completely alone.

That briefing experience was the greatest eye-opener for me. These men were making decisions, life decisions, based only on intellect, not intuition, not feeling; and they were all programmed to believe exactly what they were told. If they had stopped to feel, they would immediately have seen that Vietnam was wrong. But they didn't.

My ex-husband was furious that I spoke out the whole time I was married to him. He kept saying, "You can't say that. You can't do that." Well, I'm not going to sit there and let somebody tell me something is right when it's wrong. Of course, women have always been quiet about their opinions, which is too bad. There is no problem we couldn't solve if everyone just sat down and talked everything over together.

I didn't say much when my son decided to go to Nam, but it was obvious he made that choice because his father was so gung-ho about the military, about army discipline and all that macho crap. The night before my son shipped out I tried to talk him out

of going because I thought the war was very wrong, but it was too late. I told him that if he didn't want to go I'd help him get out of the country and we'd go live in Canada. He said, "I don't know why I have to go, Mom. I don't have any complaints against the Vietnamese, but obviously God wants me to go and I have to find out why."

He was drafted, of course, but he didn't have to go. The reason he went was because he didn't want to be a failure in his father's eyes. Well, I know there is no such thing as accident or coincidence, so I knew it was his time to go. God led him over there to learn something from it, and used it as the way to get my son back "home."

When he shipped out on October 15, 1970, I asked in a meditation if he was going to be all right. My guidance, whose voices I can hear very clearly when I meditate, told me, "Your son will be killed before March 1st." It was a terrible thing to know, and I was very sorry I had asked because by that time he was on his way and there was nothing I could do to stop him.

I called a friend of mine who is a Yogi and I told him that my son was going to be killed and wondered if I could take over his karma, his debts from a previous life, onto me, so I could die instead. My friend said, "Oh, no, your son is going to be fine." He told me to surround him with the Christ light and chant a powerful mantra, which I did constantly, but on the 12th of January, he was blown up in a minefield.

When the two military officers came to the door to tell me, I was alone. I said, "What's happened to my son?" They were silent, and then I knew. I just couldn't believe them. My head couldn't handle it because I had believed so completely that what the Yogi had told me was right. I sat there in shock; there was nothing I could say, nothing I could do.

My husband came home with our other two children and when he saw the officers there he knew what had happened. Oh, I was so furious with my husband! He had spent nine years in S.A.C. telling me, "We're doing what we're doing so that our kids won't ever have to go to war."

Bullshit. My marriage ended right then, that minute. I said, "Tell me again about those nine years you spent making the world so safe?" And I walked away.

I found out that my son wasn't even listed as a war death because the number of casualties was very carefully hidden by the government. He was listed as an accidental death—accidental, I guess, because he accidentally was in a minefield!

Vietnam wasn't a war like World War II. These poor guys had been over there knowing there was no way they were going to win; and they had to sit there until they finished their year, hoping they wouldn't get blown away until then. And when they came back, they were ignored.

The suicide rate among the Vietnam vets is the highest of any group in this country, and that's because we still haven't done anything to correct it, and the government sits there and denies responsibility for the mess it has made out of peoples' lives. War does affect sensitive men. I was called in to a veterans' hospital and I lectured to the staff on some of the problems facing the Vietnam veterans, and afterwards they said, "We have such a terrible drug problem, and we can't let the public know." None of their techniques were working, nothing would after people get all psyched up to kill, kill, kill.

When we get our fill of wars, I guess we'll find ways to avoid them. How many more wars do we have to endure before reaching that point, I don't know, but I do know that it is the mothers who must stand up and say, "No." If there is anything I learned from Vietnam it is that I don't want another son of mine to go to war. I will do anything, but I will not allow my two boys to go. I will never sit quiet and allow that to happen.

Violence begets violence. Whatever you give out, you get back. If our government can't spare a thought for our own people who are being sprayed with Agent Orange and sacrificed, if they don't care about them when they send our sons off to war, then it is up to us to stop them. Somebody has got to care enough not to sit still.

Bette Howard participated in peace demonstrations and encouraged her son to file as a conscientious objector of the Vietnam War after she lost a husband and brother in World War II.

UNITED STATES

I grew up in the Main Line area outside Philadelphia with my mother, who was widowed, and with my brother and sister. When my brother was seventeen he begged my mother to sign the paper that would allow him to join the Marine Corps. She signed, and he enlisted.

I had never been interested in politics or world events. The parting from my brother when he went into the service had no great impact. I didn't wonder whether he would come back. I vaguely remember seeing the war headlines, but they didn't mean much to me.

He had a short training and was sent to Guadalcanal, and the next thing we knew we had a telegram. So quick, and yet it changed our lives completely. It changed us from a kind of protected suburban family to people with a completely different feeling about life. I had just gotten my first job, as a lab technician in a medical college, but when my brother died my mother decided she didn't want to live in Philadelphia anymore; she wanted to start completely clean and new. We sold everything we had and got on a train to Los Angeles. We weren't there a month before I was introduced to an army officer, and in six months we were married. It was like a dream, a dream of love, to have only been there one month and to have met this wonderful man! I didn't even think about his military career. I was so wrapped up in him. He was so young and handsome.

We were together about two months before he was shipped out.

I remember standing on the dock watching his boat leave, seeing him standing at the railing and getting smaller and smaller. It seemed almost like a dream, like I was someone else experiencing our parting. He wrote to me every day, every single day.

Then the war was coming to an end and I decided to go back to Philadelphia to wait for him there. One night I went to a church social. A telephone rang down the hall, and as it rang something shot through me! I knew the call was for me and that I was going to be told that Bill was dead. It felt just like an electric shock, this knowing. My girlfriend answered the phone, and it was not for me, but twenty-four hours later the telegram came. I have a very strong feeling that he died just at the time that telephone rang.

He got shot by a sniper in Luzon, in the South Pacific, a couple of months before the end of the war. I received letters from his commanding officer and from General MacArthur. They didn't help, they didn't console me. My mother had been appeased somewhat by my brother's Purple Heart medal, but I wasn't by my husband's. Nothing consoled me. I wouldn't even consider having Bill's body brought back. I would never have visited his grave anyway, since he wouldn't be there. He's in my heart, in my mind. Someone you love lives in your memory of them, and you can't mourn over a piece of ground.

At first I thought maybe there'd been a mistake, that he hadn't been killed, but then they sent me all of his clothes and belongings and his wedding ring. It took me a year before I could cry. I was just numbed by the violence of his death. I couldn't mourn openly, like you're supposed to do, but that didn't mean I wasn't grieving.

Shortly after my husband died I decided to volunteer at a veteran's hospital. I felt I had to put sorrow away from me and get on with my life and contribute something. I felt a bond with the veterans, and that I could help them to live through what they'd experienced and show them that people do care and that there is love in the world.

I never felt anger at men in general because of war. I blame the five or so people who rule the world and who consider us nothing but cannon fodder for their wars. Money, power and greed control the world, and nobody could convince me otherwise. I was

brought up a Catholic, but I'm not anymore. I don't even believe in God anymore. There can't be a God when there is so much devastation in the world, so much pain!

It was after my husband's death that I started to pay attention to headlines. I wanted to know what they meant. I had to know what was going on in the world.

After seven years, I remarried, and believe it or not, my second husband was a Marine. I have no idea why I married a man in the military again. We even lived on a base surrounded by military people. Looking back, it seems as if I must have been crazy to have plunged into that kind of life, but I was so busy with the three children I had that I didn't think very much about it. It was social and peaceful then, in the fifties; I never thought about the possibility of another war. Finally I divorced my husband and raised my children on my own. I had decided from the moment they were born there would be no violence in my house, no violent television shows, no toy weapons, no guns, nothing that would depict war—I offended many people by shutting off a television show if there was violence in it. I tried to subdue what I felt, but I couldn't. Grief and anger simmered in me for so long, and violence would make me hurt so that I couldn't stand it sometimes. Though violence was out in the world, I decided it wouldn't be inside my home, as well.

The sixties were a difficult time to raise kids: drugs were on the scene, parents weren't as strict as they might have been, and families were splitting up. I was working eight hours a day and still had to hassle with my children when I came home at night; but, eventually the fights got fewer and fewer. I had a number of talks with them, hoping to inject thoughts into them as to what war really is, that there's nothing glamorous about it. I hoped that it would make them think twice about wanting to fight in the event of a war in the future.

So, along comes Vietnam, and my oldest son was high on the lottery list. When we discovered this, I took him aside and said, "Roger, I cannot allow you even to consider going into combat, even to join up with the army at all. I will do everything in my power to get you out of this country, but you will not go and fight!" He felt the same way I did. Many of his friends were getting shipped out, but my son decided to try to get a Conscientious

Objector status. He wrote letters and went to people in the community who knew him, and presented all this at a hearing with his draft board. He was mailed his C.O., which was almost unheard of. I was so happy! He had to do two years in the local hospital, swabbing floors for minimum wage. I was bursting with pride that he had the guts to do this when so many of his buddies had gone to war.

When my youngest was about ten, I went on my first peace march. I'll never forget that day as long as I live. Thousands and thousands of people were there. I felt as if I'd been released from jail. I felt that there were other people in the world who felt as I did, after all. I think I floated all those miles. When I got back on the bus I felt something cold coming through my shoes, and I discovered I had worn the soles off and never even knew it. If only the world could get high on that kind of thing, instead of violence.

I think women in general are too accepting. We accept too much from the world without protest. In many ways war controls our destiny, changes our lives forever. I had been a member of a close family, but because of my brother's death we felt the need to move to another part of the country, and then had to try to put our separate lives into some kind of order. We never were as close a family again.

I think in a sense all people who go through tragedy hide themselves behind a curtain, and sometimes they peek out to see how it feels outside, but they don't want you to get too close because it might hurt. Their wounds aren't bleeding anymore, though they will never be healed. I am somewhat that way, myself. Even today I can be driving along and suddenly these things hit me: my brother, my husband, and it's like somebody put a knife in my heart. It actually aches. It still aches.

Rozan Perry was married to a soldier who left her for a Vietnamese woman; he was later bayonetted to death by American youths near his base.

UNITED STATES

When my husband first got orders to go overseas, he was really very upset. I don't think he wanted to go, but he ended up spending eighteen months over there.

After his first trip home, he told me he was going back. We both cried. He said, "It's not as bad as I thought it would be." But his letters were horrible. He'd confide in me the way he would've confided in me had we both been home. He'd just write whatever he felt or thought and send it to me, and I never told him that these things upset me because I was afraid he'd stop writing, or make his letters short and unreal. It bothered me terribly while he was over there because I knew his lifestyle had changed considerably. I don't think he got into drugs, but he was lonesome. I know he stayed with other women. I more or less accepted that. It's a hard thing for a man to go through, being away from his family, and so I pushed the jealousy out of my mind. We didn't talk about it, but he knew I knew.

Living over there and coming home were two different worlds for him. Over there he was almost a completely different person. Over there he was with the rest of the guys and did all those things expected of a "macho man." I think he had a lot of trouble with himself, fighting with the feelings that he had.

When he was due back, we went over to Travis, and after I got over there I didn't feel so bad—there must have been thousands of military people leaving to go on these transports, like something out of a multimillion dollar movie. There were thousands of soldiers in lines all over the place, and crying children, wives and mothers and fathers all crying.

Things started to change. His letters got shorter, which really hurt me. I thought it was maybe something I'd said or done. They got fewer, and he started just to ask general questions, like, "How's Matt? I wish you'd send me some pictures of him. I feel like you don't say much of anything about our son." There wasn't any love note at the end of the letter. He'd just sign, "Milton." I got to the point where I didn't want to open the mailbox. I had a feeling something bad was going to happen.

Finally, he wrote me and told me about this woman he was in love with and asked me for a divorce. I wrote him, "You can't have a divorce while you're in Vietnam. When you come home, if you feel the same way after your tour is over, I'll give you a divorce."

He moved back home and we talked about the whole thing. Not because I'm sadistic but because I felt I had the right to know just where I stood and what his plans were. He said he had met a woman over there, had gotten her pregnant and wanted to marry her. He felt sorry for her and her family. He was very young and impressionable, and I guess this really ate on him. Maybe he felt that she needed him more than Matt and I did. It was like he had one foot in each world. When he was with us he felt for us and knew what his life was like and remembered how it had been before he went, and it had been good enough that he wanted to return to it. But once he got back there, I don't know whether she had some kind of hold on him, but his life just went crazy. Everything was fine when he left again, and we were looking forward to him coming home. He got back over there and the first letter I received was, "I changed my mind. I want a divorce."

When he finally returned to the U.S. for good, he was given a thirty day leave before he was to report to his new duty station at Clovis, New Mexico. He asked if he could stay with Matt and me a few days. I said, "Sure, come on back." Though he slept on the couch, everything seemed normal again. Then, he had to leave for New Mexico.

According to police reports, he had been in a Clovis bar, and was giving a ride to "an itinerant farm worker." The car wouldn't start, so my husband asked a group of teenagers if they could give his battery a jump. Evidently they said something like, yeah, if he gave them some bucks. My husband said, "No, I'm not going to

pay you. You either do it or you don't." Words were exchanged and the boys went away angry. When they came back one of them had a bayonet. My husband and the other man locked themselves in the car but the boys broke the windows and stabbed my husband to death in the car. The other man jumped from the car and ran, but he only got about two hundred feet until the boys caught him and stabbed him to death too.

I went back to work. We tried to carry on a normal life. It was very hard. It hurt. My heart ached, literally ached, it felt like a hard knot. I'd lay in bed at night and think to myself, "This is never going to quit. I've never hurt this bad before." But finally, the pain started to go away a little bit at a time.

I felt my husband, and any other G.I., had no business being in Vietnam. I was not a protestor during the war, but I had strong feelings that we had no business being over there. I relish my freedom, but I would like to live in a peaceful place where I know that when my son grows up, if Matt has to go to war, he'll go to war for a reason, not for some stupid piece of paper that says, "Well, let's try out this new bomb today," or, "Let's give the economy a shot in the butt."

It's too bad this country has always been run by men. They don't watch the children grow, and they don't watch them die. They have a very low mentality when it comes to human life, and I'm very sorry to say that. I think to myself, they say history repeats itself. Well, my father-in-law grew up and went through World War II. His son grew up and went to Vietnam. My son's going to grow up, and he's not going to go to war unless it's here in the United States. I don't care whether it's in Europe or China or Russia, I don't care where it is on this planet, unless it's on our own United States, I just will not see him marching off to war.

GAIL NEUHAUS

Gail Neuhaus struggled with the effects of her career-military father's alcoholism, violence, and sexual ambivalence.

UNITED STATES

My father came from a poor family that was trying to farm an area in Colorado that couldn't be farmed. He's a misogynist. He hates women and has no sons. I think I was a son to him, actually.

My father's first assignment was in the Philippines and Indochina in 1928. The scars from that were alcoholism and occasional family violence. He beat my mother. She didn't take that for long, and left. It meant giving us up, and I realize she had to go—she was running for her life—but it hurt. She fought for us in the courts, but the war was on his side. The military took care of him, and he got custody of us. I ended up living at the Presidio in California with him and my sister.

He wasn't cruel to me. As a matter of fact, if he had been just a cruel person then it would've been easier just to hate him and stay away, but it wasn't like that. We would go to Chinatown to have supper, we'd go to the Japanese gardens. Every day I would be taken on a walk to the Legion of Honor, if not by him then by one of the several housekeepers we had who came and went.

He took me to Angel Island, where he was arranging some sort of training for the military buildup in Korea, and to several army bases where I was treated like a princess by the men. They even had a little miniature combat uniform made for me and my sister got an officer's uniform. I got the combat uniform and I'm the one who resisted Vietnam.

I lived for awhile with my mother in Nevada when my father was in Korea, and my mother was very antiwar. She was against

the atomic tests in Nevada, and very few people were against them in those days. People labeled her crazy for being against them. So I had her influence too.

When my father was in Korea he had a mistress and children, and he'd send us photographs of them. What happened to them when he left? Soldiers come, they propagate children, they leave. It's ancient. It's been going on for centuries. To me, things like that are caused by an archaic part of the brain that keeps people from being civilized.

I lived with my father again when I was a teenager. By that time he was totally alcoholic, a drunk. I paid his bar bill one winter and it was ten thousand dollars. He had had the shakes for years, but now he'd run a fever, as well, and would go into detailed descriptions of very gory scenes he'd been involved in—terrible violence, like so many of the men either witnessed or committed.

When I was older my father was jealous of anyone I associated with. I think he was hurt and disgusted with himself, and lonely and afraid of being left alone. That's a problem the military doesn't work on, men feeling disgusted with themselves. You cannot rape a woman and shoot her and not have it increase self-loathing. I was sorry for him, because I knew under all the crap, he really loved me and I really loved him.

When we went camping he'd get drunk and tell me gory stories, and horror stories about my mother. He would go on and on about women: "They're all prostitutes." Did it ever occur to him that I was a woman? When I was nine years old it occurred to me that I was also the target of his disgust. I still have problems trusting people in love relationships, but I'm getting better.

It wasn't pointed out to me until 1970 that it was him who was sick, not me. I had taken it all on me because I was German and thought his kind of brutality was genetic; and my father often would say very Nazi, very fascist things. Of course, these were common things to hear in the military. If you don't have a uniform on, you're suspect. It's another world entirely. At least he never had any ideas about glory, I'm glad about that. He never presented war to me as glorious or what he did as glorious.

I've gotten to see things from a wider perspective. I still visit my father and listen to the stupid things he's done with his life. Last week he told me about once laying a minefield and then having to

get back across it, trying to remember exactly where he had put the mines. I thought, "You asshole." He has that kind of machismo, that pride in having done stupid things, a total disrespect for his own body, let alone for the whole earth.

When I lived with him as a teenager, he was a Sergeant Major, and he did training, and a lot of men came back to see him. They really cared about him, and there was a comradeship with them. He always had a younger man close to him. I mean, there are so many homosexual implications in it. The love they felt for each other—if only he could have lived it in a romantic way instead of in this horrible, repressed, disgusting way. I think his love for other men is a beautiful thing, just like I think his love for me is a beautiful thing. It's a shame he cannot fully express his love to me or to other people. He's so alone. ... And we just keep on laying those minefields instead of learning how to be together, and at peace.

Margaret Kilgore, Saigon, 1971.

Ruth Smith, 1977.

Marian Shelton, with her husband, 1962.

General Dinh visits all-women guerrilla unit in Mekong Delta, Vietnam.

Peggy Tuxen Akers, with veteran Ron Kovic.

Kathy Kane, front right, with other stewardesses.

Peter Forman Maker ran dangerous missions in the French Resistance during World War II; she was forced into hiding in England, and later joined the French army.

FRANCE

We were in Versailles when the war broke out. I was eighteen and a student, as was my younger sister, and my mother was a teacher. My father had left us many years before. We were British subjects, although my father was French and we lived in France since I was a baby. In 1940, schools were closed down and my sister and I began working in refugee centers where people came from the north of France, fleeing the Germans. We fed people, changed babies' diapers, calmed people down and got them on their way. They were in a pitiful state. My mother, who had been in the first World War, encouraged me to take nursing classes quite early on so that I could help when the war got very bad. She knew what happened in war; she had seen it. She had also told us to buy lots of food, so we had stockpiled a good supply of staples at home—rice and noodles and flour and sugar—and we had enough to survive on for quite a while.

Our house was on the outskirts of Paris, and my sister and I had to ride our bicycles into the city every day to the refugee center. One day we were riding in to work and we saw big posters nailed up everywhere that said Paris had been declared an open city and there would be no fighting, but that the German troops would occupy it the next day, the 10th of May, 1940. We just turned our bicycles right around and returned home and told my mother and the neighbors that the Germans were coming. I felt very angry and helpless.

Normally the town of Versailles had seventy thousand people living in it, but the next morning, as the Germans began march-

ing down the streets, only seven thousand people were left. Everybody else had taken off. My mother was too sick to go, so there was no question of our leaving the city. Through the slats of our wooden shutters we watched the Germans goose step down our street, and for two days we did not go outside.

Many of the private homes on our street were occupied by the German Army. One hot day our windows were open, and a German officer calmly stepped through one into the room, announcing that five men would be billeted with us. I said, "Over my dead body, you are! My mother is sick and no one can be billeted here." My mother heard this commotion going on and came downstairs, putting her hand on my shoulder to calm me down; but I said, "You'll have to find somewhere else to put your men. And now you go, and not through the window this time, through the door." I think he must've found it funny because he laughed and apologized and left.

People returned to their homes with many tales of atrocities: how German planes would fly down low over the roads full of refugees and machine gun them down. This stiffened my resolve to have nothing whatsoever to do with them.

The German officer whom I had told to leave started coming to our house with some of his men bringing food with them for us to cook. My mother felt that if we didn't antagonize them, they would leave us alone; so, she was friendly to them. My sister sat with them, too. I stayed in the kitchen because there was no way I was going to sit and eat with them.

In the beginning the Germans sent the French to do their dirty work. One morning a French inspector and two policemen were at our door to take away Mother to be interned. They went upstairs to help my mother with her suitcases and told us they would be back in two days for my sister and me. I was too numbed to feel much of anything after they had gone.

Some very good friends told me that we should leave the occupied northern part of the country for southern "free France," which had not yet been occupied. We left for the train station with our passports stuck in our boots and nothing but the clothes on our backs. I knew we had to get to the British Consulate in Nice, and that was all I thought about. When we finally got there, the Consulate arranged for some money to be paid to us every month.

I joined a Catholic organization of working girls and stayed in a convent. We were given knapsacks and a pair of shoes and other things. Then we were told to leave because the area was to be used for German defenses and would be out of bounds. We bought a map of France and tossed a coin on it and it landed on Grenoble, so that is where we went.

We stayed there in a convent, and I decided to become a nun and join the order that had befriended and sheltered us. My sister went back to England, and I went to a convent in Lyons, where I tried to convince the Mother Superior that I had a calling; after a brief novitiate, they tried equally hard to convince me that I hadn't, and they won. But they gave me a room in exchange for working in one of their schools.

A priest who was in the underground asked me if I would take false identity papers across town, after curfew, to a convent. They would be given to young people who would otherwise be transported back to Germany. I told him I couldn't because I was terrified of being alone in the dark. With the blackout, it was really very dark. He said, "Well, it's up to you. Fifty lives depend upon it."

I thought it over and decided that if it was a case of one life against fifty, I'd better go. I took my rosary and the false identity papers, and went. I never said so many Hail Mary's or made so many signs of the cross in my life! From that time on I continued to do a lot of praying because I smuggled a lot of false documents. Many people decided their lives were worth that risk; it was just something we had to do. When the Germans came marching down the street, I knew I wanted them out.

We couldn't do anything, men or women, on an individual basis; it all had to be organized and orchestrated, and be very exact. Violence against the Germans was impossible since any act of violence by the French would result in retaliation. Some German soldiers were killed in a small town not too far from Paris, and all the women and children were herded into a church which was then set on fire, burning everyone in it to death. We could not risk that kind of thing happening.

I got more involved in the underground, smuggling identity or work papers for Jewish people or people who faced deportation or forced labor, or for people who needed to get over the border and

didn't want to use their own identity papers. A girl whose father was a collaborator with the Nazis and worked at the City Hall would sneak into his office at night and put the official seal on all the false papers. There was no way we could duplicate that seal, though we could duplicate everything else.

There had to be much secrecy in the underground for it to survive. We only knew the person immediately above and below us in the organization, so if we were caught and tortured, we weren't able to give much away.

One day a girlfriend and I had some papers to deliver. We were on a streetcar when the Germans stopped it so that we could all be searched. I couldn't stay on the streetcar to wait for my friend in case the Germans got suspicious about why I was waiting, and so I went on home. After a while there was our secret knock on the door and she was there, just laughing her heart out! I was shaking, thinking she had been caught. She said, "Do you know what I did with the package? Did you see that soldier next to me with his knapsack open? I put it in there!" There were no names or photos on them yet, so we weren't endangering anyone by getting rid of the papers the way we did. My friend said, "Can you imagine his face when he opens his knapsack tonight? How will he be able to explain that to his commander!"

I communicated with our friends in Versailles, who wrote to me that they had been able to reach my mother in Vitel, where the Germans had surrounded some hotels with barbed wire and were using them as an internment camp. There were two thousand women in there, half of them English and half American. One day I managed to get an Ausweitz, a permit to travel, from the Gestapo commander of the camp where my mother was. The first time I went to visit her I had a few butterflies in my stomach, wondering if the paper I had was sufficient. I wasn't scared, but I was worried. A young man sat opposite me on the train and we had been told the train would stop at the border for no more than ten or twelve minutes. But when the minutes kept passing, it became apparent that the Germans had halted the train for a search. I looked up and the young man across from me was white as a sheet. I whispered, "What's wrong?" and he said, "I haven't any papers." I said, "Act as if you're looking for yours and let me give them mine first."

The Gestapo finally got to our compartment and I pretended to be looking very hard for my paper while they were looking at those of two other people in the car. When they asked us for our papers, I kept pulling out documents, saying, "No, this isn't the one. Wait a minute, here it is! No, that isn't it, either," while the Gestapo was becoming more and more impatient, getting ready to haul me off the train. Finally I pulled out the real one and said, "Oh, here it is!" just as the train whistle blew. They looked at my paper and left.

In a little villa just outside the camp's barbed wire where people could meet with their visitors, Mother arrived wearing a cape with many pockets inside. Although they were allowed to give us two cans of food from the Red Cross, my mother had cans in every single pocket. When people had heard I was coming to see her, they had saved some of their food rations too. My mother told me to be prepared to be given much more food the next day, and so nuns at the convent made me a cape full of pockets. When I came out I had enough food to fill a suitcase, and cigarettes too, which I could sell on the black market.

Every six weeks I got an Ausweitz, so I would pick up the papers and maps and whatever I had to deliver, visit my mother, and then go on to Paris and drop them off. I did this for two years.

As the war went on, travelling became more difficult and dangerous because thousands of people were going from place to place and because the trains were being bombed with increasing frequency. The trains were so crowded that going to the bathroom was a big problem; although men, who could go out the window, only had half a problem. Women would just have to go in their pants.

One time my mother told me that the camp commander was going to allow the internees to have a picnic and I could stay the whole day. Everybody was very anxious to know what was going on in the outside world because they didn't have any radios or newspapers, and I told them the news. This gave them hope because by then we felt the war wouldn't last forever and that the Germans were losing. It was important for the internees to have hope because many of the women, young girls especially, suffered, with no place to go where they could be alone. They would get very despondent; there were a lot of suicides.

However, women thought up things to pass the time. My mother, who was a wonderful musician, organized an orchestra with some other women, and they somehow obtained instruments and arranged classes. She had always wanted to play the cello, and the camp commander, who played the cello very well, taught her how to play. After the war, quite by accident, I found out that he had been working for British Intelligence and knew what I was up to all the time.

One day he called me to his office and told me there was to be an exchange of sick internees in Portugal where four hundred British would be traded for the same number of Germans, and that he wanted my mother to be in that exchange. This was two months before D-Day. He said that my mother's health was too precarious to risk her staying in France, but that she couldn't leave without me. I must've looked at him kind of suspiciously because he said, "I know what you're thinking, so why don't you go back to Lyons and ask your boss what he thinks of the idea of your going to England?"

I was very confused and very suspicious, and I wasn't at all sure that I understood what he meant by my "boss." He gave me another Ausweitz to come back to camp, and I left for Lyons. By this time I was having to change rooms every two or three days because the Gestapo was very much on my tail. One time when I was in Vitel visiting my mother, there was a knock on the door of my bedroom and a mother superior stood there, white as a ghost. A Gestapo officer was standing behind her. He walked in, clicked his heels and saluted, "Heil Hitler." I jumped out of bed in my long flannel nightgown, and he said, "Is there a man in here?"

"There's no man in here."

He checked the cupboards and under the bed and between the mattress and the springs, behind the curtains, everywhere, then turned to leave. At the door he clicked his heels and Heil Hitlered me again, and then said, "Have you ever heard of Peter Forman?" Quickly I thought, "He thinks he's looking for a man," and I said, "No, I don't know him." And he walked out.

You see, the Germans followed orders to the letter, and the fact that that Nazi believed Peter Forman was a man meant that he would only look for a man and never consider the possibility that

Peter could also be a woman's name. However, on the chance that he might have the bright idea to ask if Peter Forman could be a woman, I packed up immediately and left Vitel.

The priest, back in Lyons, said to me, "Look, we aren't going to be able to use you anymore because it's getting very dangerous. If you go to England you could do more good than by staying here." I went to Vitel.

I had to stay six terrible weeks in that camp, then we finally were repatriated. The train was supposed to take three days and nights to take us from Vitel to the border, but it took fifteen days and nights because it was right after D-Day and the bombing was incredible.

When we finally arrived at a bombed area that was on the border of Spain, the Vitel camp commander turned up and told me he was going to lock me up in the toilet until we had safely crossed the border. "Say nothing to anyone until you are in Spain," he warned me, explaining that I wasn't on any exchange list, but was allowed on the train on his orders. I assumed, since I was the only person on the convoy who wasn't sick, that he was trying to get me into Spain safely, but I wasn't at all sure why. He stood outside the door of the toilet and German soldiers would come to the door and rattle the knob and he would say, "I checked it," and they would go away. Then the train started again and I knew we had passed the border, and when I came out of the toilet the Vitel commander was gone.

We felt good about reaching Spain, but in every village we had rocks thrown at us because the Spanish hated the British; and we were glad when we finally got to Portugal. There was a reception at the British consulate, at which we all wore our torn and filthy clothing, which prompted them to buy us new clothes the next day. A Swedish ship took us back to England.

It was wonderful to be back in England, and to see my sister again, but I was too restless to sit back and do nothing. Women had joined the armed forces in large numbers, so I went to the British War Office to join too. The officer in charge there told me, "Look, it's late. By the time we get you trained, the war will be over." He gave me a letter to take to the French headquarters, telling me that I'd be of more use to them than I would be to the

British, and so that's how I joined the French Army. I entered as a lieutenant and was put in charge of repatriating people who had been deported by the Germans.

I worked first in England and then I was sent on to Paris, where I discovered the Nazis had stolen all of my mother's possessions. I went on to Berlin and then to the tiny town of Aroslen, where the International Tracing Service was headquartered. All the documents regarding deportations were gathered there, and it was my job to issue Presumption of Death certificates so that survivors could remarry, or whatever they had to do to get on with the business of living the rest of their lives.

I found out so much about what had happened during the war from those documents. The Germans had kept very good records about where people had been sent and what work they were given to do or what medical experiments were performed on them. One Jewish woman I read about was pregnant, and they tied her legs together during labor to see how long the baby could survive if it couldn't come out and to study what her reactions would be. They both died, of course, and that too was efficiently noted. It was like a nightmare reading those papers.

We knew very early on what was happening in the concentration camps, just like we knew what the Butcher of Lyons was up to. At first our information came through the underground, and later, when we had so many occupation troops in France, we heard more. I never could understand how German civilians could say they didn't know what was going on; it seemed quite idiotic to me since we knew what was going on and we weren't even in Germany. However, after the war, when I was working in Germany, I stayed in a house which was near a small concentration camp just outside town. The owner of the house had been allowed to stay in it if she would act as a maid, and one day I took her over to the window in my second floor room, which had a clear view of the camp, and I said, "How can you deny what happened in the concentration camps when you can see inside one from your own window?" She said, "I never saw it."

I couldn't believe this at first, and then I thought about my friends who had accepted the German occupation of France and had done nothing about it. I realized that people really do not see things they don't wish to admit exist, that it is easier for them

simply to deny what is unpleasant by not "seeing" it.

After the war, the sound of the German language being spoken really bothered me. It brought back such terrible memories. When I was first married, I remember my husband putting on the radio one Christmas. Suddenly I got goose pimples and had this feeling of imminent danger. I was absolutely rigid with fear. Then I realized it was because there were German songs being played on the radio.

Later, even though I could not watch anything about the war, I still had my family watch, so they would never forget what happened. What hurts the most is that so few people remember and so few seem as if they really would protect and cherish their countries against the kind of things that happened in World War II. I am afraid that if it could happen again, it would, because too few people would help to stop it.

Once you have heard enemy boots marching down your street, you become very aware of what people are capable of doing to other people, and you change. What happened once can happen again, and if it can happen to one country, it can happen to another. A lot of people don't realize that all this I've told you happened only yesterday. We dare not forget that it could also happen tomorrow.

HANNA VOIGT

Hanna Voigt, daughter of a German spy and wife of a Nazi general, rode courier between bombed towns and acted as midwife and medic.

GERMANY

My father and mother weren't around when my brother and I were growing up, and we didn't see much of them at all until they came back to Germany in 1925, when I was fifteen. Most of that time all we knew about them was that they were in the United States, but we found out later that my father was acting as a spy for Kaiser Wilhelm II. He blew up several places important to the U.S. Government, including an ammunition depot. Many horses were being shipped to England during World War I, for the cavalry, and they had to have shots before the trip. My father posed as a veterinarian and gave shots to a shipload of them so that they would all die on the way.

He had been a trusted friend and advisor of the Kaiser and of President Hindenburg; and he was involved in the international meeting at Den Hague to discuss what Germany owed the United States for the damage done in the war. He owned a shipping company and business was very good after the war, especially business from the American friends he had made.

Things went well for us and we owned a big ranch, where we raised thoroughbred horses. I started out riding, and I became the leading jockey in Germany in 1927. I raced until I was married, in 1932, but my husband didn't want me to continue. I began jumping and steeplechase, instead, and later did cross-country, at which I was never beaten.

My father gave a lot of money to the Stahlhelm, the old German party that didn't go along with the new National Socialist party, which later became the Nazis. The party came to him for money,

too, but my father said no. He was very angry when Hitler was appointed Chancellor. Slowly Hitler managed to have our foreign contracts cancelled, and business got worse and worse. One day, while I was working as his secretary in his shipping office, my father came to me and said, "I have to go to a meeting and I don't feel good about it. If I'm not back in one hour, come to Hillman's Hotel and ask for me."

He didn't come back, so I drove into the city to the hotel and asked the concierge where my father was. He told me, warning me also that there were a lot of Nazis with him. When I got upstairs I found two S.S. men standing on either side of the door. I told them that I had to go in and talk to my father because something important had come up, and before they could say no, I was already inside.

I'll never forget the picture of my father, sitting at a desk with an S.S. man on each side of him, and a revolver lying in front of him in the middle of the desk. My father stood up and picked up the revolver and said, "You see, Hanna, they want me to shoot myself," and then he threw the gun out the window. I said, "Come on, there's something important I have to tell you about," and we left. The S.S. men were so surprised that they didn't know what to do.

After that, though, my father was frightened, and soon he decided to take a trip to Spain. My husband, who went with him, told me afterward what happened. First the ship radio malfunctioned and the operator couldn't seem to fix it. My father, who had learned how to do things like that when he was a spy, went into the radio room and had just repaired it by the time a steward came in with a cup of coffee. My father said, "Thank you, I think I earned this!" He drank it and then fell dead. It was a terrible, sad thing.

The police force became part of the army and so my husband was ordered, in 1934, to the poison fog detail. He was sent to the place where the Nazis were experimenting with ways to kill people. They would have people walk over electric plates and be electrocuted or put them into a gas chamber, trying to find out which way would work better. Hitler used retarded people in these experiments so that he wouldn't have to feed them anymore, and also because they wouldn't know what was going on and try to escape.

Several officers, including my husband, had to put on gas masks and go into the gas chamber with some of the victims so they could see for themselves how well the poison worked. For some reason my husband's mask didn't work right and he swallowed a little bit of gas. He was taken to a doctor, and when he had recovered they sent for me, telling me he had an infection. My husband didn't tell me the truth about what he had seen until the war was over. Even when we heard about how people were getting killed in concentration camps he said he didn't know anything about it.

At first my husband was not a Nazi. The man I married was a nice man, but the war years changed him. For instance, there was a rule Hitler made that if an officer's wife didn't have a baby within five years of their marriage, then her husband should divorce her. I thought it would only be a matter of time before he got rid of me.

Two years later I got pregnant, and I had the baby shortly after the war broke out. After not having children for seven years, in the first four years of the war I had five! My husband would come home on leave and I'd tell him, "Keep your pants on this time!"

There was a big parade in Nuremberg—at that time we were living in Fulda—and my husband, who had been put in charge of heavy artillery for the army, had to go and arrange the section that would be presented before Hitler. They had the parade and then when they were loaded up and ready to return home, they were told, "You're not going home; you're going to the French border."

I waited for him, but there were no telephone calls, no messages. I didn't know what had happened except that all the officers from Fulda were gone. Finally we heard on the radio that they were on the Belgian border, where my husband then crossed over into France.

After four weeks I got a letter from him, but there was no way I could write him back and let him know that at last I was pregnant. It would have made him so happy, and I was afraid he would get killed and never know about his child.

I decided to help the Red Cross, which made it easier to refuse to join the Nazi party. Many German women who lived along the French border were being evacuated and they didn't want to leave their homes, so many of them had to be taken to the train by force. Pregnant women and women with babies were evacuated first and

they would pass through on cattle cars and stop at our station.

Many times the train would pull out and we would find babies lying on the ground where their mothers had thrown them out because they couldn't care for them or thought they were better off dead. Many women would throw themselves off the train while it was moving.

I helped care for the babies that lived—I sometimes had six or eight of them in my house, along with my own babies—and I would help women give birth in those dirty cattle cars at the train station. The train would stop so we could feed them, and sometimes a woman would say, "I can't go any farther! My baby's coming!" I had spent all my life around animals, so I knew what to do when the babies came.

At first we were lucky in Fulda because there was no bombing, until one of our planes shot down an enemy plane nearby. Then all of the flights going over us from west to east would bomb us. There were some nights when hundreds of people were killed. Phosphorus bombs would set things on fire, and people would be lying dead in the streets, burned black and as small as children so that you could fit maybe ten adults in a wheelbarrow.

My husband was promoted to Colonel and put in charge of Dijon, France, then transferred to the Russian front, where he marched on Leningrad and was shot in the leg. When the wounded were brought home, the train got stuck in the snow and my husband got pneumonia. I had to go to the hospital where they finally managed to take him, and I brought him home to recuperate before he was sent back to fight.

I had started riding as a courier, carrying messages from town to town, because the telephones and telegraph were so often bombed. I carried messages for the Red Cross and others, often riding as far as twenty miles and back in a day.

Many times the enemy would spot me and circle down to fire, but I think the time I may have come closest to getting shot was when I was riding a message cross-country and an enemy plane spotted me and machine-gunned around me. I hid with my horse in the shadow of a big tree until he gave up and flew away.

That day my mother died, burned to death by a phosphorus bomb which landed on her roof.

A very short time later my baby girl, who was nine months old, got sick. I was giving her her bottle and suddenly she let the bottle

fall and was dead. A couple of weeks later my son, who was two years old, went into convulsions. I called the hospital again and again and begged a nurse to come and she said, "How much meat can you give me?" I told her I didn't have any; all I had to give her was eggs, and she said, "I'm not coming for eggs, I have enough of them."

She came two days later, and I'll never forget what she did. She took my son up in his little bathrobe and held him away from her like he was something disgusting. She said, "He has an infectious disease and must go to the hospital, right away." He died two days later. I was ready to give up, but I had my other children to take care of and I had to stay strong for them. There was no choice.

Finally, the war was over. My husband, who was by then a general, had been caught between the Russian and English forces, and since no one wanted to be caught by the Russians, my husband went to the English and surrendered his two divisions. The enemy wanted to have a hearing and put all the most powerful Nazis on trial. My husband had been put on a plane with the other high-ranking officers when he was traded for a British officer and sent to Hamburg.

When the Americans came in to occupy the part of Germany where I was living, they took over my stables and made me manager. I had to teach soldiers to ride so they could do border patrol or become mounted police involved in the division of Berlin.

Part of the American camp was for prisoners of war, so I would sneak in sometimes to see if my husband was there. Then, one day a train arrived and two M.P.'s escorted my husband off. I couldn't believe it. He had changed. He had always been a jealous man, but now he was worse. He knew I was working for the Americans, yet he was jealous of every American I had to speak to. I had to work—I had children to feed and my husband no longer made a salary—but he hated that I lived in the camp and he was not allowed inside.

Sometimes he would visit me secretly in the night, which was dangerous because he could have been shot. He would come into my house and make a scene. I had to keep my mouth shut, even if he hit me, because if anyone found out he was there, they would put him in jail.

I got off one day every two weeks, and because the railway sta-

tion was far away, I rode my bicycle home to see my family. In my suitcase I always brought any food I was able to save because there wasn't enough for my children to eat. I came home later than usual one day, because I'd had to push my bike through the snow, and my husband thought I wasn't coming. I found him in bed with the housekeeper, and that was it! He tried to get me back, but I refused to return.

When we got divorced he told the judge that I had forced him into another woman's bed because of my refusal to have any more children, and the judge divided our children between us. My husband never let me see them again.

ELIZABETH WEIDENBACH

Elizabeth Weidenbach, half-Jewish, eluded S.S. squads in Augsburg, where she worked as a laboratory technician and survived heavy Allied bombing raids.

GERMANY

My father was a physician in Augsburg. I was raised Catholic because my mother had suffered very much as a Jewish girl and she thought the nicest thing she could do for her children was to integrate them with the religion of her husband.

In 1938, the night of the Kristallnacht, the Jews were first taken off to concentration camps. Up until that night I didn't know I was half Jewish. It was a very disturbing morning when a maid came into the dining room one lunch time and whispered something to my older brother, who suddenly got up and left the room. When he came back he told me that someone had written "Saujude" on my father's brass nameplate outside with black crayon. The word means "pig Jew." It turned out to be quite a typical word used in Nazi Germany.

As a half-Jewish person it became increasingly important for me not to stand out in any way: no tennis playing or riding horseback or anything that would be too noticeable. I was six years old when Hitler came to power and it was easy at first to accept the restrictions as "things we just don't do in our family." I grew up under many such restrictions.

My brother and I were on vacation in the mountains when war broke out. All the adults were very nervous and excited, listening to the radio about how Hitler had marched into Poland. We got a telephone call from home telling us we should get home immediately. Already there were soldiers and girls with flowers at the depots, and a lot of singing and excitement. It was overwhelming. Everybody seemed very intent and preoccupied with themselves.

My first taste of war was on my birthday in 1940. A friend of mine and I went to the symphony. The music had just started when the air raid sirens went off. Some man came on stage and the musicians stopped playing. "We're having an air raid," he said, "and everybody should go home in an orderly fashion." My friend and I waited underneath a railway bridge where we could see the bombs exploding. It gave me a very helpless feeling; it was all so completely beyond my control.

Then my cousin and aunt and uncle all went to concentration camps; close friends went too. When I learned about all this, the war really started hitting me, and I tried to tell the girls at school about the Nazis and about how people were going to concentration camps, and they sort of believed me but they also felt that Germans just wouldn't be capable of doing things like that. I also always enjoyed telling jokes, and there were some terrible Nazi jokes going around. I would always get carried away and tell them, and then I would lie in bed at night and pray to God that I had told the jokes to decent people and they wouldn't report me.

It was frightening when people you'd grown up with just dropped out of sight. The Nazis were very clever about that. First they took the Jews away from their own homes and put them all together in one part of town, so they lost contact with their neighbors. Then, when the Nazis came to take them off to the camps, they hadn't become friendly yet with people who could have helped them. That's how the Nazis could get away with it so easily.

You had to greet the Nazis you saw on the street with the Heil Hitler salute, but it was better for me to avoid them if at all possible and not call attention to myself. When I was fifteen and in the fifth year of high school, all the nuns got thrown out and the town's biggest Nazi became our principal. That was a very traumatic change. Instead of prayers we said "Heil Hitler" before and after class, and the principal taught us "Modern History," which began with the birth of Adolph Hitler. He would tell us how marvelous Hitler was, and I remember he would get very close to me and stare at me with these pale blue eyes, trying to see if I was making a face or disbelieving him. I quickly learned to be very much on guard and show nothing I felt. We were a well-known

family in town because of my father being a physician, and so he knew that I was "not pure."

People began to refuse to walk on the same side of the street with me. My father was changing too. He used to talk about medicine to me. Then, when I was about fourteen, he had a girlfriend who was very vicious and she told him things about me that were untrue. Gradually, he grew to dislike me.

Sometimes I would wonder why I was stuck with my mother's Jewishness, all the problems and pain that it caused, especially since she never seemed to care very much about me. If we had been close, then maybe it would've been worth it, but we weren't. What she did was like what the Catholic Church did later, when its members were having trouble and it did not provide the support we needed. For my mental survival I couldn't keep letting things affect me very deeply. After a while I didn't feel hurt about much of anything.

In 1943, Hitler made a proclamation that anyone who was half-Jewish couldn't go to school any longer, nor could poor children who couldn't pay the tuition. I was crushed to have to leave. I loved school, even with Nazi teachers, and I couldn't picture my life without it.

It was necessary by that time for anyone partly Jewish to either take a job to help the war effort or go to a concentration camp. My father had a friend who was the director of the city hospital. I became an apprentice lab technician at age sixteen. I was taught how to do urine and stool and blood tests, and I got to like the work. I worked twelve hours a day, six days a week, without pay.

The English bombed during the night, as I remember, and the Americans bombed during the day. One time the railroad which I took to work was machine-gunned by the Americans and all the people on it came to the hospital with at least two or three bullets in them. It was the most nightmarish thing that happened in the whole war to me, with all those people moaning and screaming and dying all around me. I wasn't a nurse, so I was really helpless.

The number of air raid alarms increased in 1943, until we were having to get up every night to go down to the basement. The night of February 25, 1944, we were bombed. We could hear the bombs exploding all around us, and when the lights went out and plaster fell off the walls and ceiling, we knew our house had been

hit. The men tried to get out, but the exit from the building was blocked.

The adults decided that since we couldn't get back upstairs, we would have to break into the building next door, which was a big department store. The men took the hammers and broke through the wall, and then they all escaped, leaving the women to gather up their children and follow along afterward. By the time we got into the store, it was completely burned out. My father was the only man who had waited on the other side, and we all ran through the block-long building, afraid of it falling down on our heads. When we were outside, we ran around to our street through three feet of snow, and saw our building was on fire. I felt so overwhelmed. It was unreal—the fires made the night as bright as day.

We were standing there on the street, trying to figure out our next move, when men came running past yelling, "They're coming back!" What the enemy did was to drop phosphorus bombs that were so hot when they exploded that everything would melt and burn; and then, when the city was in flames, the bombers would come back and drop other bombs on the then-visible targets. The Nazis had put these big cement tubs full of water beside the streets because sometimes when their houses were bombed, people would run out of their basements, but the sidewalks would have melted and they would sink into them. Sometimes they burned to death right there and sometimes they managed to throw themselves into one of those tubs of water.

We ran over to hide in the basement of the house across the street from ours, and the bombs exploded with so much pressure that we were thrown across the room. It wasn't a very deep basement, so the pressure simply picked us up and moved us. Many people were killed this way, thrown against stone walls.

When the second bombing had stopped, I said to my father, "You're going to have to start your practice up again, so we'd better go back and try to get your EKG machine and your microscope." I told my mother it was much too dangerous for her to go into the building, but I told my father and brother what to save. Everybody did what I told them to do, which even that night was amazing to me. My father had always told me what to do, not the other way around.

135

Our whole apartment was full of smoke. I walked across that very familiar room to where I knew the microscope was always kept, and I found it; but there was so much smoke that I couldn't find my way back. Then I heard my father's voice calling me, and I got out by walking toward the sound.

It didn't look like there were too many fires in the part of town where my father's brother lived, so we went there next. But his house had been burned down too. Everyone had been told to make arrangements to go stay with someone in the country, and because my father was a doctor and allowed to have a car, we drove out of the burned city. The snow was black all around from the fires, and I'm sure we would all have burned to death if it hadn't been there. Leaving the city I saw the sad spectacle of people leaving on foot through the black snow. One woman had a chamber pot on her head—they all had some pitiful thing—but I think the one that touched me the most was a woman who carried a shopping bag with three empty clothes hangers in it.

We got to a cafe belonging to my father's patient. We kept on going to work as usual. It never struck me that life shouldn't go on as usual, and I was too used to doing what I was told to think much about it. My parents' marriage deteriorated completely and my father decided to go back to live in the city. I remember how relieved everyone living at the cafe was when he left. Life was calmer without him and all the arguments. He stayed married to my mother until the end of the war, though. If he had divorced her she certainly would have been put in a concentration camp.

As the war went on, fewer and fewer people dared to come by our house or acknowledge that they knew us. We were getting hungrier and hungrier because of the food shortage and we ended up eating potato soup for the last two years of the war. We were only allowed two hours of fuel a day, even in the wintertime, and so we were very cold most of the time. Every day I lived with the fear of being taken to concentration camp, and I knew enough about them by then to have visions about what it would be like. I'd have nightmares about gas coming out of the showerheads.

In January, 1945, the man who had hired me called me into his office and told me that he had gotten letters from prominent Nazis that I was "undesirable" and should be fired. He said, "I've kept you here for a year and a half, but you must understand that I

have a wife and children and I can't take the risk of keeping you here any longer." I told him I understood completely, and I left.

I was in a very vulnerable position, not working for the war effort anymore, and I was frantic. I had to be careful not to be seen. My father transferred some of his patients to a private Catholic hospital and asked them if they could find work for me. They said they could, and I was very much relieved. I worked at all kinds of things: giving shots, assisting in minor surgery, sometimes even giving anaesthesia.

I remember one man who had surgery. When he started to come out of the anaesthesia he raved and raved about the Nazis and how much he hated them. Nobody would declare themselves because of the danger of being turned in to the Nazis, so it was so wonderful to hear this man's real anger. It was such a relief to know I wasn't all alone in my feelings.

It was a time of great insecurity and bizarreness. I was German, but I knew what the Nazis were doing—children denouncing their parents for being anti-Nazi, the Jewish persecution. But then the Americans and the British, who were really the people who could liberate us from Hitler, were bombing us from the skies. That was bizarre, trying not to get killed by either side. It was hard on the nerves, getting hit from every direction.

Toward the end you would hardly ever see a man anymore. All males between fourteen and seventy were drafted. There were no young men anymore, they were either at the front or dead. The bombing was so bad in Germany that there was a saying, "Cowards go to the front," because it was easier to be fighting than just be a sitting duck.

After a severe bombing, you get this terrible instinct to run home to see if your family has survived. Once there was a terrible bombing outside the hospital and another technician and I decided to go home. We weren't really needed right then, and people understood that we had to go check on our families. When we got to my companion's street, it was littered with pamphlets that had been thrown from the American planes, and she wanted to read one of them but I warned her not to. My cousin had gone to concentration camp for reading a pamphlet.

When I got home and saw the building was still standing, I thought, "This time it's safe." For some reason that day I felt the

need to see if my father was safe. When I told him about the pamphlets on the streets, he told me to go out and get one. Not until much later, not until he died, did I really understand how much I resented him for asking me to do that. I knew that if someone caught me with it, I wouldn't be going home. I went outside and found one, hid it in my stocking rather than my pocket, and went back down the street to my father's. When I got there I pulled it out and there was nothing important written on it. I had risked my life for nothing. My father and I went into the bathroom and flushed it piece by piece down the toilet, until the last shred was gone.

The rumor went around in those last few months that the Nazis were going to shoot any of us who were part Jewish because they didn't want any happy survivors. I was haunted by a film I had seen about the Nazis pursuing a spy and then shooting him in the back. I still remember how much the sight of that gun scared me, and when I heard that rumor at the end of the war, I immediately thought I would be shot in the back one day soon. I could almost feel the gun in my back. For about eight years after the war, in fact, I had nightmares about a gun at my back, and I would wake up screaming.

At the same time, there was increasing danger of being shot by the enemy. At the end of the war when we stood in line for food, the Americans machine-gunned anybody who stood in the street. I wasn't about to die to keep my place in line, and I would go take cover in somebody's doorway. The interesting thing was that a lot of people didn't move—they were so hungry they just couldn't lose their place. They were mostly women waiting to get food for their families, and they wouldn't leave. I admired them. They were desperate, but stood there with very blank faces.

The news began leaking out that the Americans were getting closer, as were the Russians. People were listening to English radio, and I remember there was a lot of discussion about how it would be better to be liberated by the English or Americans rather than the Russians.

The war was almost over. The last three days there was a lot of shelling, and the noise was terrible. Around six a.m. of the third day, the shelling stopped. It was so peaceful that my brother and I fell asleep on the sofa.

We never actually heard the war was over that day, but we knew

it was because everything was so still. We just sat and waited. At ten o'clock that morning, American soldiers started marching up the streets. They didn't look very military; they were wearing scarves and things, and no hats, and they weren't goose stepping. It was a shock to see them, they were so different from the only other army I'd known.

At noon a soldier came to the door and said that by the order of the American Government we were to give him all our camera equipment. A sergeant and two corporals searched our house for German soldiers, and the corporals got up on mother's bed and stretched out on it in their dirty uniforms. The sergeant was a nice man. "They're very tired," he said. "I'm afraid they've been up for three nights."

The hospital that had kicked me out for being "undesirable" called me in May, 1945, and said, "We have all these concentration camp survivors and we need your help." They had people from all over: Greece and Poland and Czechoslovakia. They spoke Yiddish, a German dialect I learned quickly, and that's how many of us could communicate. I took care of a whole floor, just me and a very old nun, and we made a hundred beds twice a day.

They were all such pathetic human beings! Many of them had survived the loss of entire families. Even though they first saw me as just a German, they were not antagonistic toward me. They were remarkably free of bitterness. When they found out I was partly Jewish any strain between us disappeared. Whatever we had gone through, we were all very happy to have survived.

I had really wanted to survive that damn war and the damn Nazis, and being angry helped me do that. I was very angry inside, and I often thought I could have killed them with my bare hands if ever given a chance. But the minute the war was over, that anger evaporated.

What also helped me to survive was a kind of toughness. I had learned a great deal trying to do everything my brothers did and I got hurt in the process. I was trained that women are secondary, that I was "only a girl." My mother would tell me, "Women can't afford to be moody," but I could never reconcile myself to it. I think that's why I was such a tomboy when I was young! I never had a knee that wasn't bloody when I was growing up, and I think in a way that toughness, that refusal to give in, helped me to survive.

ANNEMARIE BACHHUBER

Annemarie Bachhuber was a typist for the Nazi high command; with the arrival of occupation forces she lived by her wits, eventually escaping into the Western zone.

GERMANY

I went to a Roman Catholic school when I was growing up, and the nuns didn't approve of Hitler's German Youth group, so I refused to join. I wasn't fond of the Nazis and their ideas, and though my father was in the police force, he didn't like them so much either.

As for the Jews, I have nothing against them. My parents even bought their home from a Jewish family that was going to Palestine, as it was called in those days. That family had a son who was bigger than I was, and one day I was building a castle in the sand and he came stomping through and ruined it! That's what put a hate into my system against the Jews!

When the war started in 1939, I was sixteen. My mother had been dead over a year. My father married a woman I couldn't stand, so I moved out and my father got me a job with the police and an apartment. I started working in a typing pool, then I got transferred to ballistics. There I worked with a man who lived in Spain. Because of his political outlook he had been put in a concentration camp when he came to Germany on a visit. He was sometimes let out of camp to help me translate English and Spanish ballistics information. He was married to a Spanish woman, but one day he told me he was going to get a divorce and marry me as soon as he was let out of the concentration camp for good. He promised me heaven on earth and told me to wait for him.

I got him out of camp. I had a little camera and I took pictures of him, and then I stole an identification card and typed it out and then stole the stamp to mark it. He promised me he would find

me when the war was over, and then he disappeared.

When the war ended, two friends and I took off for somewhere safer than Berlin. We were hoping the Americans would take over, but they stopped at the Elbe River, and the Russians came in. We hated the Russians. I had saved all my morning slices of bread and roasted them so they were dry and hard and I could chew them. I packed them along with a very few clothes, leaving the rest behind including the accordian I treasured. I'd knitted a double-sided sweater which was my own invention! It had a zipper outside and then a secret zipper inside, so I could fill it up with things I wanted to keep safe—my birth certificate and my mother's and sister's photographs and some documents.

We started walking, and we walked and walked! We got closer to Hamburg and found a church that had straw on the floor where we could sleep. There were many people there sleeping, fully clothed. It was a terrifying time! We did not know what the enemy would do, and we had heard so many stories. The first English soldiers, the Tommies, arrived, and we were so hot and thirsty that I begged one, "Could we please have a little water?" He acted like he didn't understand me. I said, "Well, don't you understand?" He said, "Yes, but you're a German. I won't give you any water." I don't know what happened, maybe there wasn't any water. Maybe the enemy poisoned it so that Germans couldn't drink it.

We walked on further to where the American soldiers were camped. They were nice and said, "You know, we're not allowed to talk to you," but they gave me some salt for cooking, and they gave us some candy bars because we were hungry. They tried to flirt with us, too, as raggedy as we were looking in those days. But then I was barely twenty-two at the time. We became good friends with three of them.

On the 8th of May, 1945, we were still sleeping in that church. All of a sudden someone said, "The war's over." My friends and I and the American soldiers we had met were all so happy!

From then on life was a little easier. We decided we might as well go back to Berlin, my friends and I. We walked every day thirty to forty kilometers. Oh, it was so hard! All three of us had dysentery and head lice and body lice. Every step of the way we were itching and miserable.

I went on alone to Berlin, leaving my friends in Hamburg. Berlin was terrible. Dead Russian and German soldiers were still lying in the streets among the ruins. Nobody had a chance yet to bury them and since it was June, and hot, the bodies had started to stink. It was awful. I was still a young person, and though it was good the war was over, there was no happiness. There was still this damned depression and nothing to look forward to, no hope, nothing. I lived for three months after the war in a kind of coma. Nothing seemed real anymore. We still weren't safe because the Russians were occupying Berlin. They were dangerous and I tried to stay away from them. I went back to where I had left my clothes before leaving Berlin, and they had all been stolen. Shoes and clothing were very hard to get, so I took apart burlap sacks and knitted sweaters out of them and then I made more to sell. I made a little bit of money that way, but not enough to live on.

I met an Italian who had lost his wife and child in a bombing in Italy. He had the intention of marrying me, but while I liked him as a person, I could never have stood him as a companion for life. Besides, I was engaged to that man I had saved from the concentration camp. He helped me because I had no money and no job. When we found an ad in the paper for an accordionist, he took me to someone who had an accordion so I could play for him. He said, "You play wonderfully! Why don't you make money with that?" He gave me the two thousand marks to buy an accordion, which I later paid back, and I made my living after that playing at the Picadilly Club.

It was a beautiful, sophisticated nightclub. I started at six o'clock and I played until two in the morning, making more money in tips than what I got in salary. I knew all the popular American songs and could play them all by ear. That pleased the American soldiers and officers who came in. "Pack Up Your Troubles" was a typical war song, and "Oh, Yes, My Boy, Will You Dance With Me?" I remember one Russian officer who came in one night and asked me to let him hold my accordion and show him how to play. He put a large banknote, a hundred marks, down my blouse. I was dressed very nicely, of course, with my hair all in curls.

I really had a good time there and I made good money. When I had saved enough, I brought my sister and her baby to Berlin on a

cattle train. We both got into the black market. While I worked at the club, she made lots of hard liquor from caraway seed, and sold the bottles for a thousand marks each! The Russians liked it because it was hard for them to get vodka. We made a lot of money, so that when my sister finally heard from her husband, she returned to live with him.

I was alone again, working in the Picadilly Club, when I got a letter from my fiancé, sending for me to come to Munich and marry him. When I left Berlin I was told to take the train up to a certain village, then walk towards what we called the Green Border, through the woods from the Russian occupied country to the American side. I had only a small bundle with me, and I was wearing that double-sided sweater with my mother's picture, some documents and a beautiful silver knife inside.

We were a group of about three men and four women, and we headed toward the western side through the thick woods. Very soon we were all caught by Russian soldiers. Oh, we were so frightened! They took us to their camp, but then they let us all go. We thought then that it would be better if we split up. I was the only one to get to the other side alive.

I was so scared and my mouth was so dry that I had to lick the icicles on the trees. After I had lost my sense of direction, I just kept on walking, hoping, and then suddenly I looked up and saw two Russian soldiers in front of me! They grabbed me and took me to their camp and locked me in a barn. Every ten minutes another soldier came in and raped me. To look unattractive, I scraped my fingernails down my face so it was all bloody, but it didn't do any good. I was thirsty and I asked a soldier please to give me some water. He gave me vodka, which made me sick.

The commanding officer was a Mongolian Russian who looked at me with stabbing eyes. "You're a spy, aren't you?" he said. I told him no. Suddenly he saw my silver knife shining through my sweater and said, "What is this? Give it to me!" I had to unzip the secret inside zipper and give him all my papers and my last and only picture of my mother, which he tore up in front of me. He found my school diplomas and discovered I could speak French, English, Spanish and Italian, and he cried, "You're a spy! Look at all the languages you speak!" He held a pistol to my head, and I remember thinking, "This is the end."

He didn't shoot me. Instead he took me up to his room and raped me. I was worried that he would find the money I had, but he didn't. He took me downstairs and told two soldiers to take me out in the woods and shoot me. When we were hidden by the trees, they talked for a minute, and then one of them went back to camp. The other one threw me in the snow and raped me. Then he showed me directions where the Americans were and let me go. By that time I almost didn't care anymore if I were alive or not. But I was so afraid of getting caught again that I lay down in the branches of a snowy fir tree, and it seemed like I lay there on the snow for hours and hours.

Then all of a sudden I heard roosters crow and some life going on. I heard shouting. I looked up and thought maybe the sounds were coming from the American side, but there was a wide open field between me and the buildings. I was scared to go because it would be so easy for me to be seen and shot. I was so frozen, though, I decided I had to take the chance.

I went as fast as I could across the field, thinking every minute I would be shot, and I reached the fenced yard of a farm. I yelled, "Hello, somebody there?" A door opened up and I said, "Is this the American side?" And they said, "Yes." They gave me a chance to wash my clothes and give myself a sponge bath, and they gave me coffee and some food. Then I asked them how I could get to Munich. They told me there was a truck that passed that would give people who had escaped a ride to Munich for thirty dollars.

When I got to Munich, the driver told me how to get to where my fiancé lived. At first he acted very romantic and then, the next day, he sent me to some friends of his for new clothes, which I paid for myself. It was from these friends that I found out he was going to get married, but he was not going to marry me. He was going to marry this "housekeeper" that he had known from before he'd gotten in the concentration camp. I couldn't believe that he would betray me like that.

I found a room and moved out. Then I told him what I thought. He said, "The nigger has done his duty and he can go," meaning that I had saved his life and he had gotten me out of Berlin to repay me, and now our relationship was over. He didn't need me anymore.

I never went back to Berlin. I stayed in Munich, first making

leather buttons to earn a living. Then I started working for the Americans in their Special Investigation Section. That was where they interrogated suspected Nazis. I typed whatever was said during the interrogations.

In 1955 I met my husband, who was an American soldier. We got married the following December. I always wanted to explore another country of the world. By that time I was over thirty and thought that if I didn't marry then, I never would. I didn't love him, but I thought we could adjust to each other and be happy.

I didn't have anybody left in Germany, anyway. My father was involved with his third wife and his young children, and my sister was married and had her family in Austria, and I was alone. I was really alone ever since my mother died. Always on my own two feet and putting them down and standing up by myself! I had rough times in my life, but I always came through. People thought they could get me, but they never could. I'm a tough German!

SARA FABRI

Sara Fabri was deported from Hungary to the Auschwitz concentration camp in the last year of World War II.

HUNGARY • GERMANY

I went to Auschwitz on a train from the detention camp where we'd been kept in Hungary. My father and mother were both with me in the boxcar, which we shared with so many people that it was difficult to sit down.

It had been awful with the Germans occupying Hungary the last three months; but, I suppose it hadn't hit me as hard as the adults, who had been worrying about how to keep their families from being deported and how they could go into hiding, which very few managed to do. I was fourteen years old, but it wasn't due to my age that I didn't know what was going to happen; most of us were unaware of what was awaiting us. The Germans had made a tremendous effort to keep things secret, and so we had only a vague idea that what we were going to was just another internment camp.

Before Auschwitz, before the knowledge of Auschwitz, you couldn't have believed there was such a place and such calculated cruelty. There were rumors, but no one believed them. They would say, "This can't be true; this is the twentieth century! Germans are people, too, and this is nonsense." We thought it was just crazy wartime propaganda.

I first saw Auschwitz on a bright summer morning, June 29, 1944. There was a brilliant summer sky. When the train stopped and the boxcar doors were opened, all the sun and light and air were overwhelming after the dim airlessness of the boxcar. There were many German soldiers standing there and some people who looked like convicts, in striped uniforms. Things moved very fast then. We were told to leave our few possessions behind, that we

would be given them later. We had to get out of the boxcar quickly and I remember milling around in the crowd, not seeing much but the taller people around me. I remember how gray everything was. In the distance there were rows and rows of barracks as far as the eye could see, and they were as gray as that dusty, dusty ground. There was a great deal of shouting and pushing and formations being arranged. It seemed to be very chaotic, but evidently it was all finely calculated. The German soldiers and the men in the striped uniforms, in no time at all, separated the men and the women. They kept shouting, "You will go to the showers now, and you will meet your family again in the evening." After three days of being in that boxcar, the idea of having a shower was wonderful. Somehow the word "shower" was continuously in the air.

The men in the striped uniforms told us they were prisoners like us and that everything was all right and we shouldn't worry, but just stand where we were told. All of us were very tired, and I don't remember a great many details, just all that milling around and then finding myself suddenly in a group of women with my mother. I don't remember in all that chaos the moment we were separated from my father.

I am sure that our arrival was a calculated psychological assault and that whoever had planned it must have taken into account our tremendous fatique and confusion. Everything went so fast, being ordered here and there, people crowded tight against you and the dust rising up high around, and the Germans being so efficient. That incessant reference to showers—somehow it had all seemed so logical to take showers and meet again later, that we just obeyed. One of the things I feel very bad about is that I don't remember in that chaos the moment I was separated from my father. I was very close to him and loved him very much. I never saw him again, and I don't know how or when he was killed.

The next thing I remember very clearly. I was standing in the road with my mother and a group of adult women. It was a very stony road, flanked by barbed wire fences, beyond which were ditches. There was an SS man guarding us for a long time. I guess we must have been put through the selection process without my having noticed. Beyond the fence were barracks on that gray ground, and between two of those barracks we saw a group of

147

people, creatures.... They were wearing women's outfits but they were bald and didn't look like either men or women. They were behaving in a strange manner, squatting on the dusty ground or loitering, looking incredibly bizarre. When they saw us they began to wave and holler in our direction. They evidently wanted to tell us something, but we couldn't hear them. Then a woman with a stick ran out and chased them away. The SS man who was standing there with his gun and who had up until that point said nothing, suddenly remarked, "Those poor creatures are lunatics, but they are being taken good care of." We believed him.

We were marched off, and the next thing I remember was being in a low-ceilinged room that was very long and smelly and damp. Some women came in who were dressed in striped outfits, and they had their hair and looked all right. They started telling us that they were prisoners, too, and had been there for a while and that we shouldn't worry, that the labor was hard but the treatment was fair; and, of course, though families would work separately, they would all be able to live together in the barracks. The fact that they had been in Auschwitz for years and seemed fine was very reassuring. Also, since this was toward the end of the war, after D-Day, it was clear by then that the Germans were going to lose. It was terrible to be imprisoned at the last minute, but we had the feeling that if we could just hold on, we would survive.

One of the women in a striped outfit came up to my mother and asked, "Is this your little girl?" and my mother said, "Yes," and the woman asked, "How old is she?" and I told her I was fourteen. So the woman said in a pleasant way, "Then she'd better register down at the far end of the room. Adults work but of course children don't, and it's better to register at the very beginning so there's no mix-up. Later you'll be together again, of course, in the evening." What she said made sense and my mother told me to go register. There were other girls down at the far end of the room, two of whom I knew from school at home in Hungary. The woman told us all to go into the room next door, and we did.

Then she slammed the door behind us and started to scream, "Undress, undress! Take off everything, everything!" She had been so pleasant in the other room, but this behavior was calculated to destroy us. It was so humiliating to undress in front of everyone,

but by then it all seemed just like one raving nightmare. The combination of confusion, embarrassment and fatigue, of sleeplessness and hunger made it impossible to realize things clearly.

I took off my clothes and then another woman grabbed me and pushed me down on a stool and began to shave my head. All I remember about that, looking back, is how the metal felt gliding over my head. I remember getting up and wading through all that hair on the floor.

I've always tried to pinpoint the moment everything took on that air of terrible unreality, whether it began with the sight of those strange scarecrows who had shouted at us or not. But by the time my head was shaved, nothing seemed real any more. We were totally unprepared for what was happening to us.

They pushed us into a shower room and then into another room where they threw us filthy dresses. Mine was the size of a tent and the shoes were mismatched. I had one flat-heeled shoe and one high-heeled shoe; both of them were far too large. Then we were pushed outside, where we stood waiting. Somehow, all that day we were always being pushed somewhere, marched somewhere, and then left to wait in a group.

By this time the feeling of unreality was total. I looked around at all the freshly-shaved heads, waxy white and extremely strange. I saw two creatures standing there, and one had the face of my girlfriend Eva and the other had the features of another friend called A'gi. These girls I had known all my life, but these bald funny figures looked like they were wearing my friends' faces like masks, as if they were faces that didn't belong to the bodies wearing them. We hugged each other and laughed hysterically.

Again we were marched on and I had a terrible struggle walking in my shoes, and I couldn't take them off because the stones in the road were so sharp. We were herded into a barracks, which was very dark, lit by only a few skylights in the ceiling. There were three tiers of immense shelves down each side of the room and an aisle ran the length of the room to the large front doors. We were told to get up on the shelves and stay there and be quiet. We climbed up on those splintery planks and waited.

We were sitting there when the front doors were thrown open and in came those bizarre creatures we had seen on the road right after our arrival. I remember that was a moment of absolute panic.

They ran in and climbed up on the shelves next to us. Close up they looked even more like lunatics than they had at a distance and they were stinking like hell.

They weren't lunatics; they were Hungarian girls like us, only they'd been in Auschwitz for three or four weeks. It was then the world came down. They enlightened us. They told us they had no chance to wash themselves, and that they were hungry all the time with a hunger that ate you from the inside, and that they were frequently hit with a stick. Being beaten was part of life at Auschwitz, as I was soon to learn. Then they told us the absolutely worst thing—it was not true what we had been told: we were not going to meet with our families. We had merely been told that so we wouldn't make a fuss when we were separated. They told us the same thing had happened to them and that they had not seen their families again and had no idea if they were still alive.

It was the absolute bottom of Hell, although there is no vocabulary to describe what Auschwitz was. The girls told us it was they who had hollered and tried to get our attention, trying to tell us not to reveal our ages. They always tried to warn new groups when they arrived at camp even though they'd never succeeded.

Everything that had seemed unreal disappeared then, and what we faced was reality. It felt like I was falling, falling, with nothing to hang on to. All that we had been told, all the deliberate lies were now clear, and the reality was so horrible that we were in this terrible place, and we were there alone. For the first time in my life I felt totally alone. What we had vaguely dreaded had come true.

Still, even at that point we didn't give up. You cannot give up so easily those things you want badly to believe. We asked, "But those people in the striped uniforms said they were prisoners, too, and why would they lie to us?" And we were told that yes, they were prisoners, too, but they were working for the Germans. They were collaborators.

I crouched in the darkness, squeezed tightly against the other girls. It was hot and stinking with three or four hundred of us in there. I felt it was the end of everything and tried very hard to hold on to something, but I couldn't. I knew I might never see my parents again. My home was gone, and my freedom. I don't remember that I wanted to die, but I didn't want to live. My life

since then has brought me many sorrows, but never has anything been like that first horrible night.

Finally, after a while, I realized somebody was talking to me. I felt someone's arm come around me in the darkness. Someone said to me, "You want to get out of here, don't you? You want to be free again, don't you? Then you must get hold of yourself!" She kept repeating that. I don't know what I said, but it was probably something about my family and being alone, because she said, "You aren't alone. We are your family." She kept repeating these few things over and over, I don't know how many times. All I remember was that dark night and that voice and that arm around me.

Books about life in the camps will tell you that the first day and night there were crucial. That it was then you would decide in some part of yourself whether you wanted to survive, whether you could bear to wake up every morning in Auschwitz and realize the nightmare was true. You had to get up and face it, and if you had somebody who helped you do that in one way or another, it made you feel facing it made sense. I don't know if I could have faced what happened after that night without her, without that simple, straightforward truth, and her goodness to me.

What had happened that first day had made me doubt human motives and had profoundly shaken my belief in my fellow man, and what this girl did for me balanced all that. Not only did she help me to survive, but helped me to survive with my belief in humanity. And this was absolutely the most important thing— because survival itself is not enough. It's how you survive. And if you survive knowing that even if there are some bad people, there are very many good people and many in between. That life is of many colors and shades and that you can't let the cruel affect your view of life. This girl was the first of many to help me realize this.

Basically, what it came down to was that even at fourteen, one had to question human values. People discovered, after their naïvete and ignorance were shattered, that people did exist who were indeed capable of terrible atrocities. That people were capable of greed and cowardice and unwillingness to help Jews we had already learned in Hungary, but what we learned at Auschwitz was something entirely new. Yet people like this girl showed me that people who are mean and greedy and murderous aren't all of

mankind. In that terrible darkness, that one light made all the difference.

I wasn't just an anonymous body squeezed between other anonymous bodies. Here was a loving person beside me who bothered to talk to me, who knew what I was feeling and was willing to help. She was someone to hold on to in Hell. Many times since, when I've been in unhappy situations, I've thought of her, and she still balances with her goodness the meanness of others. To this day I can still remember the feeling of her arm around my shoulders, and though I can't recall how her voice sounded, I still remember vividly those words she repeated in my ear.

Sometime later, I must have fallen asleep. The next thing I remember was the whistle blowing and the chaos as we were driven out into the early morning darkness to be counted.

I could never find out who that girl was.

ELSA SMUSKEVICH

Elsa Smuskevich fled her native Latvia when the German army invaded; she became the youngest sniper in the Soviet army, riding in advance of the troops and killing numerous Nazis on the long Eastern Front.

LATVIA • SOVIET UNION

My family and I lived in Riga, Latvia, which was taken over by the Soviets in 1940. I was fifteen the summer when the war broke out. The Nazis were approaching very fast, but we thought the Russian Army was strong and that the Nazis wouldn't be allowed to advance very far. However, soon they were bombing the city and it was decided that my older sister should evacuate with her three children, and that I afterward would join her, while the rest of my family stayed home. Everyone thought that we would stay away no more than two days and in that time the Russian Army would be able to drive the Nazis out.

My brother-in-law had a motorcycle, and he took my sister and her children out of the city first, and then he came back for me. But when we got to where he had left my sister, she wasn't there. We were told that the area had been bombed and that all the people living there had been evacuated somewhere else. We went on, searching for her, but couldn't find her. We reached Estonia, where my brother-in-law left me for a few hours to go help someone else, and when he came back he couldn't find me in all the crowds of people who had fled Latvia.

I realized I probably couldn't find my sister in the confusion, and I wanted to be with my parents, so I decided to return home. On the way I met some neighbors of ours from Riga. They didn't want to tell me that the Nazis had taken all the Jews and killed them or sent them to concentration camps, so they told me my family had been evacuated to Russia and if I went there too, I would find them.

I was put on a train with many other refugees and taken to Yaroslavl, Russia. The trip took seven days and during that time I had nothing to eat. When I got to Yaroslavl I got a job harvesting crops for the farmers, and in exchange they gave me some food and let me sleep on the floor.

I cried day and night, so worried about my family that I had blisters all over my arms and hands and my fingernails came out. In September there was snow on the ground and it was already terribly cold. All I had to wear were the clothes on my back and a thin summer coat.

All the children from Leningrad came to Yaroslavl, and I was told to live and study with them. The weather got colder with the coming of winter. The Nazis started bombing Yaroslavl, and it was decided it was too dangerous for children to stay, so all of us were sent by train to Siberia.

It took us sixteen days to get there. I got sick because of the hunger and the cold. We traveled in cattle cars which were heated by a small iron stove. Because I was so sick, the teacher in our car put me next to the stove to stay warmer. The stove was red hot, and at one point the train came to a sudden stop and I was thrown against the stove, burning my thigh very badly.

I was hospitalized for three months. They treated me well and fed me and clothed me. I could understand Russian quite well by then, and could get along. After a year, I received word from my sister, and decided to leave immediately.

It was difficult to get a place on a train; there were people at the station who had camped there for months trying to get a seat. I got on an open flatbed with two hundred Germans who were inhabitants of Russia but were being sent deep into the interior so they couldn't aid the Nazis. Germans had lived in Latvia a long time, and I liked them—it was the Nazis I hated. It never crossed my mind that it would be dangerous for a young girl to be alone with all those men for two days and nights. They were good to me. They had had to leave their wives and children behind, and I think maybe I reminded them of their daughters back home.

I felt so lucky when I finally found my sister, but she had been very unlucky. Her husband was fighting on the front, and two of her three children had died of illnesses aggravated by cold and starvation. Shortly after I arrived, I happened to hear on the radio

one day what had happened in Riga, that 21,000 Jews had been shot by the Nazis. Not just shot, but forced to dig their own graves in the snow, take off all their clothes, and then be shot and thrown naked into the graves. I realized, listening to the radio that day, that my parents must have been among those who were killed, unless they had been sent to a concentration camp in Germany from which they might never return alive.

All I wanted was revenge. My own life meant nothing to me anymore. I thought that even if I could kill just one Nazi, I would have more self-respect by paying them back for what they did to my parents. I went to the city's recruiting office and told them I was seventeen years old and that my parents were either killed or put in a concentration camp, and that I wanted to go into the army to get revenge.

The recruitment officer told me I was very young and inexperienced and that if I joined the regular army I would be sent to the front as an inexperienced soldier and would probably be killed. He told me that I should get training first so I could be of more help to the army. So I went to the army school in Moscow, where I trained to be a sniper. We had nine hundred girls in my battalion, and I was the youngest. Most of them were fighting because of patriotism; but some, like me, were motivated by revenge.

I went through basic training and learned how to shoot and throw grenades, and how to hide from and pursue the enemy. It was physically hard for girls, especially since we did all of our training and fighting in the snow. I was graduated from the school earlier than usual because the army needed us, and we were sent directly to the front lines. I was impatient to get there. The Russian front was very long, from Stalingrad to Norway, and all nine hundred of us were spread out along its length.

Six of us were sent to the front line at Murmansk, near Finland, where the snow was more than ten yards deep. There were only the six of us there, in a camp of four hundred and eighty men, and we slept in a small wooden house. It was bitterly cold and though our clothes got wet in the snow, we couldn't dry them at night because we were afraid the Germans would see our fire.

Even with that proximity, still there was never a case of a woman in the army being raped. There were, however, many love affairs, for obvious reasons, but also because women snipers were

highly respected by men, and desired not only because we were women, but also because we were considered brave.

I met my future husband in the war, but I would have nothing to do with him, or any other man, because I had made a vow to God that if I had nothing to do with men and just paid all my attention to my job, then maybe I would be able to find my parents alive after the war was over. I had this feeling that if I did all I could to help in the war, the war would be over sooner and my parents would have a better chance. I was young and pretty and had many admirers. It wasn't difficult, though, for me not to get romantic with a man. They were only friends to me, that's all. My mind was on more important things.

Murmansk was a port city, the only port through which food and medicine and arms and vehicles from the United States and Britain were distributed. The army was there to protect the port, and our troops were no more than fifty meters from the enemy. We were placed in front of the front line, to watch what the enemy was doing and to shoot any officers or enemy snipers we saw. The sniper rifle was very tricky because it had to be carried very carefully so the sights wouldn't shift out of place. Even shaking it a little bit would move the sights and throw off your aim.

Because of the snow, everyone wore white camouflage, and it sometimes wasn't easy to locate the enemy. You could be standing there with the enemy in your sights only moments before you would be in his, and the trick was to shoot him before he shot you. Once an officer asked to look through the sights on my gun and the moment he put them to his eyes, an enemy sniper shot him in the face and horribly disfigured him. I was glad to escape that, but I knew the bullet had been meant for me and so I also felt very bad. It was also my job to locate machine gun nests on the enemy side and try to disorganize them.

I will always remember the first Nazi I shot. I was in a trench very close to where the enemy was also waiting in a trench. Across from us was a very active group of machine gunners, as well as some excellent snipers, who had been killing many of our soldiers. Our men attacked this center, but still several of the enemy were alive and continued to shoot at us. I got a Nazi in my sights and shot him.

I was glad that I was finally beginning to even the score against

them, but it wasn't like killing a human being. I didn't think of Nazis as being people. They were only targets to me. If they had been human beings they couldn't have thrown babies into the air to shoot. They didn't think at all about the horrible way they had killed or tortured my family and ruined my life, and so when I shot that first Nazi, and then all the others, I felt no more about it than shooting something less than an animal. I never thought about their lives, whether they had wives or children, and I have never regretted their deaths and I never will.

After I shot that first Nazi, they put a photograph of me in the newspapers—one many young soldiers carried around with them—first, because I was probably the youngest girl sniper in the Soviet Army, and second, because I had killed my first Nazi only a week after I had gotten to the front.

I don't remember how many Nazis I killed because I stopped counting. I was not and am not a killer. I didn't enjoy killing and I always had to tell myself that the Nazis had, after all, started first. There wasn't any time to think about the act of killing because when I came across an enemy sniper, we were face to face. There was no chance of both of us surviving. I wasn't afraid of being killed, but I didn't want to be crippled or disfigured. If my family had been killed, I had nobody to take care of me, so I had to come out of the war able to care for myself.

Once there was a bombardment with firing on both sides. I went with a group on a reconnaissance mission to try to capture an enemy officer and force him to reveal his attack plans, but before we could do that the Nazis found us and started firing. Many of our troops were killed or injured. There was a mud hut dug into the snow nearby and the injured were put inside it. I went further on down the trench to see if I could kill any more of the enemy because they were still shooting at us, and an officer saw me and told me to go into the mud hut, too. I promised him I would go in soon, but I didn't because I wanted to stay out and help. Just before I was going to go into the hut, a bomb landed on it and everyone inside was killed. All six of us girls lived through that mission, but only four out of forty men survived—mostly because they were doing the attacking while the snipers stayed behind them, watching the enemy and killing them as the men retreated under fire. I had known and liked many of the men and I

felt terrible and confused. I stood there in the snow and cried, although I did not often cry while I was in the army, only before and after.

It was a hard life, but I was young, and women are really brave. I remember several times when a commanding officer was killed, the soldiers hesitated, not knowing what to do. The women were the first to take control of the situation and help the men to continue fighting.

I cannot compare the bravery or military excellence of men and women in general. Among the snipers, I do know that men and women were absolutely equal. Actually, women are often better fighters than men because women know exactly what they are fighting for, and that makes you a fiercer fighter. A woman has to have a reason to fight, a reason to leave her home and go to war. If she has that reason she is a wonderful soldier. In my case, I wanted to show that the Nazis could be stopped. I felt that if I helped, the war would be over faster and my parents would have a greater chance of being alive. I also fought out of hate, out of revenge.

After Murmansk, I was sent to Latvia in October, 1944, with the troops that were to liberate it. I wanted to participate in the liberation of my homeland, and also I kept thinking maybe I would learn something about my family. I went to Riga and there I learned that all of our friends had been killed. I saw my house and strangers were living in it. I felt so homeless. I asked people who had already been liberated from concentration camps if they had seen my parents. But when more and more people returned from the camps, I started to lose hope. Then I was told that my parents had been killed in Riga with the 21,000 others.

I was nineteen years old. Life meant nothing to me after I thought my parents were dead; I could see no future. However, by the end of the war, I could see the possibility of a future because I was reunited with the man I had fallen in love with and there seemed to be a life for me to live after all.

My battalion had to continue on to Lithuania, and I had to go with it. Then, in May, 1945, the war was over. I was on the front when we heard the news on the radio. It was wonderful. People went crazy with happiness, singing and dancing and crying and shooting guns in the air. All I could think of was at last to go

home to Riga, but I had to remain in the army three more months, getting the last of the enemy out of the country and taking prisoners and helping people return to their homes. Then I got my discharge papers and went home.

During the war I didn't understand the risks involved; but afterwards, when I saw so many women who were missing an arm or a leg or who were blind or disfigured, I realized how lucky I was to have survived without serious injury. During the war I never thought about the possibility of what could happen to me. I did what I had to do and never thought about whether what I was doing was right or not. War made life very simple—merely a matter of endurance.

Every year I would go back to Moscow during the days when they honor their war dead, and meet with the women who had been in my battalion. The Soviet government honored the contributions of women who had fought and died in the war. I felt very proud that I had done something to help, and that I had also done something to avenge my parents' death.

It is strange, though, that I never really felt revenged. The Nazis had brought me so much pain and sorrow. I had been a lucky girl, with parents and loving relatives and a home, and in one day I lost everything and almost everyone I loved. What I did was not nearly enough to repay what the Nazis had done, but I couldn't live and do nothing.

The war changed me. Before the war I was naive and innocent and gentle, and after it I was independent and wanted to do everything for myself. I was much more nervous than I had been and more careful, less trusting with people. In Russia women are not supposed to be fighting for their rights or independence, the way they are in the United States. Women are equal in Russia and can have the same jobs as men, but still the feeling is that women should be home, raising children and dependent on a husband.

Just being a typical woman after the war was very difficult for me because I had had so much life experience and was used to thinking for myself and making my own decisions. I had my own opinions about everything, and not everybody likes that in a woman. Life was more difficult between my husband and me because we had both seen combat in war. I didn't worship him for his bravery because I had been just as brave, and I demanded as

much attention as I was willing to give. He knew what I had suffered and I expected that because of that he would give me special attention, and be more considerate, but he wasn't. He wanted the same things from me. He hasn't resented my demands, but perhaps he's resented the fact that I do think I know as much as he does about many things. He wanted to be the leader of the family and make all the decisions, but because of the war, I am a leader too, and just as capable of making decisions.

There are many changes war makes, some of them surprising to me. It is strange, but I cannot bear to watch anything about war on television, and nothing violent at all. It is hard for anyone, the violence and ugliness and sorrow of war, but especially for the young who should be spared such terrible knowledge. I see what is happening in the world, and I feel that another war is coming and there is nothing I can do about it. Maybe I will no longer be alive, but my children and grandchildren will and they will have to experience the horrible things I lived through. That thought haunts me and keeps me awake at night. I think if I had to endure it all over again, I wouldn't. I'd rather die.

MICHIKO BYRD

Michiko Byrd was forced to flee Nagoya, the third largest city in Japan, which was bombed heavily during World War II.

JAPAN

Before the war we had a good life. My father had a business, a blacksmith shop behind our house, and my uncles worked for us. Western-style living had already been introduced. My mother fixed pancakes and coffee for breakfast, we used knives and forks instead of chopsticks, my father played the violin, and we had a phonograph. One of my uncles took me to American movies, with Fred Astaire and Ginger Rogers. My other uncle was strictly Japanese, so he took me to Japanese movies. My father took me to cafés and the poolhall, and my mother took me shopping. Modern living, a life half Japanese and half American.

Then, when I was eleven years old, the war started, but I was too young to know what was going on. Since we were living in a big city, there were air raids. In the beginning it was just once in a while, but Nagoya, where I lived, was an industrial city, the third largest city in Japan, and so soon they started coming to bomb the factories.

In Japan, people stay where they are born, and they die there. But the war made me move from place to place and it was so confusing that finally I didn't want to go to school at all. They were teaching us English, and I thought, "Why in the world do I have to know the enemy language! I hate it so much." Then, in the second year of the war, we were sent to work in the factories to help make parts for airplanes and war machines. It was fun; I didn't have to study. Mother packed us food for the day, and when the air raids came we would go down into the shelters and eat. It was a happy time; I didn't feel that war was so terrible. All I felt

was cold when the air raids came, sometimes all night long, and we had to get up out of a warm bed and go into the cold shelter. That's what was hard, I think, for young children, that and not enough food to eat. A handful of rice would have to be stretched to feed a whole family; we added more and more water until the rice was mush, and then no rice at all, just cloudy water. We had to eat every bit of the vegetables; the eyes from the potatoes and the stems and leaves, nothing could be thrown away. Even to this day my mother will never throw rice away.

We were burned out of our house twice. It was the kind of bomb that just burns, very fast. Fire went onto our roof and my father went up to put it out, but it was too late. We put towels over our faces and we were screaming, and my mother had to get all six of us outside. She couldn't be frightened herself, she had to be strong, with six children. There's an old Japanese saying, "Woman is weak, but Mother is strong."

We decided to go to our grandparents' house, which was in a little fishing village. My father had to stay behind with the other men to take care of the city—they couldn't abandon it—but he came to visit us once a month and bring my mother money. The village was right on the path to a big city, so we had air raid warnings there too, everytime the B-29's would pass over.

My mother told me about how she learned never to trust people anymore. One day when the airplanes kept flying lower and lower over us, she was frightened and tried to take us into a shelter that somebody had built underground. She begged and begged them to let us in until the airplanes passed, but those people refused her. She was frightened for her six children. I see a scar in her attitude right now, even the last time I visited her I tried to get her to eat fresh rice, but no, she held on to the old rice until it was gone, held on to the old memories of being afraid and not trusting.

One thing I can see now is all the propaganda we got from the military dictator, Tojo, and how all the so-called "little people" had their minds filled with, "We are disgraced by the United States, we have to show our strength!" We didn't have any doubts; we didn't take a minute to think what it all really was about. I had no doubt we had to have war. Before that war, there was a war with China, and we were always told that we were winning. Every time we supposedly took over another city, we had a big

celebration. Gradually we were brainwashed into thinking we could win, even against a big country like that.

Everybody was overjoyed when the war was over, but what hit us most was that we were defeated. We were sad to hear the Emperor tell us that, to hear that he was crying. We were a country of no defeats, a polite and proud country.

I was happy going back to Nagoya where I was born. Everybody was scattered though, because my city had been burned to ashes. We went back to where our house had been and there was nothing but weeds. I remembered how my old room had looked, where my desk had been and all the little things I loved, and I stood there on the bare ground, kicking a stone with my foot, not knowing what to do. I went back to school for a little while, but everything was different.

We automatically accepted that Americans would come and occupy us. At first we were afraid that all the American soldiers would rape the young girls, so we were shut inside our houses. We had all pictured the soldiers before the occupation as having great big Jewish noses and red hair, eating big bloody steaks, and we called them "Yankees" the same way we were called "Japs." Then the Western culture started coming in again, and I could go to the movies and see Gary Cooper.

Looking back, I fell sorry for that girl who was me, sorry for what she went through, but I'm an optimist. I won't let problems or crises change me into a negative person. I experienced things and learned from them—with God's help! I never became a victim, war didn't leave me with a deep scar. I don't know what other people felt about the war now because we don't talk about things like that. Oh, maybe men do, but I think men talk more about war because they think more about the past. Women think of tomorrow. My attitude is, the past is past. I want to live today and tomorrow because today is another day and for tomorrow I have hope.

SHIGEKU SASAMORI

Shigeku Sasamori watched as the atomic bomb fell from the American B-29; she is one of the well-known "Hiroshima Maidens."

JAPAN

During the war we would hear about other cities being bombed, and though we could sympathize with the people who had experienced that, we really didn't know what they had gone through. We were almost relaxed about our life in Hiroshima because it had never been bombed. We didn't really think we would be bombed, either. Very often B-29's would fly over, and we'd just point at them and say, "There goes a B-29." Interested, and not very scared.

I was a student in junior high school toward the end of the war. Most of the younger students were out of the city, in the country staying in temples or living with relatives. Older students, along with adults helped tear down and remove houses in order to widen a few narrow streets in the event we had to evacuate the city quickly.

The morning of August 6th was clear and beautiful and sunny. My girlfriend and I were walking to where we were supposed to work cleaning up the street that day, and along came a B-29 over- · head. I looked up and pointed and said, "Oh, look, a B-29," unafraid and pleased to recognize it, like a child. Then I saw something white drop from the plane. I had no idea what it was. I was remarking on it when the bomb exploded.

Everything was immediately red and black. The force of the explosion knocked me over backward. I thought, like everybody else did, that it was just a regular bomb, but that it had dropped very close to me. Before we knew to call it an atomic bomb, we called it "Pika Dono," which roughly translates as "flash of fire and booming sound."

Have you ever looked inside a furnace? It was like that all around me, all red with fire. I started to get up, but I was knocked down again. I remember that I wasn't scared but just very surprised by what was happening. I didn't realize I was burned, but I knew I wasn't dead, and so I wasn't afraid. I could hear nothing and I felt nothing. Some people said they heard the explosion or saw the mushroom cloud, but I think because I was so much inside the blast, right under the mushroom cloud, that all I experienced was the explosion.

I was determined to stand up, and by the time I was standing all the redness was gone and everything was dark and gray. I looked for my friend but she was gone. I don't know if she was conscious sooner than I was and had gone or if she had been blown away by the blast, but I never saw her again. The air was full of a kind of fog that was slowly clearing away. After a while it was clear enough so that I could see people moving. They were black with ashes and their clothes were torn and they were bleeding. Many of them had skin hanging from their bodies where it had been almost torn off.

I followed people away from the center of the city, which was lucky, because many people did lose their way with all the buildings gone and walked toward where the bomb had fallen instead of away from it. Most of the people that morning had been cooking breakfast when the bomb hit. After the houses were destroyed, the cooking fires began to burn in the ruins, and soon much of Hiroshima was in flames. Many people who were not killed by the bomb were burned to death in the fire.

I followed the people to the river outside the city, but still didn't feel anything. More and more people were coming from the city behind us. Here and there I could see smoke rising from the fallen houses. The air got clearer and clearer, not clear like it was before the bomb, but clear enough to see. I guess the mushroom cloud was disappearing. People were pushing forward into the river, to try to stop the burning pain and to escape. I was afraid they would push me in.

Suddenly I heard something—a baby screaming. Its mother was trying to get it to nurse at her breast, trying to comfort it, and both of them were burned and bleeding. Then I heard other people moaning and screaming and crying, but most of the people were

165

silent, walking along like they were ghosts from hell.

Somebody said, "Let's go to the other side of the river," thinking there might be more bombing. I couldn't tell how to get home, and my school was on a hill on the other side of the river where people wanted to go, so I followed along. We crossed a bridge, which collapsed later that day and many people crossing it were drowned. I don't remember how long we walked but we could see some of the school was still standing, along with quite a few houses. People came out to give us what little water they had and to help us. Someone put oil on my hands and for the first time I felt the pain. I looked down at them and the skin was all wrinkled and dark with ashes. I realized I couldn't move my head or neck, but I couldn't see what was wrong. I sat down under a tree and as soon as I leaned my back against it, I lost consciousness.

After some time I could hear peoples' voices and sense many people around me, but it was so dark that I couldn't see them. We had been moved into the school's auditorium which was lit only by candles. I was there for four days without food or water or medical care. Day and night I dreamed of such a beautiful place, with a sky that was full of a golden light much more beautiful than sunshine and a wonderful blue ocean and a fountain that shot water high into the air. I dreamed of drinking water, I was so thirsty. It was so bright and so beautiful, that I think now I was in heaven all of that time. Such a bright, shining place! When I came back to consciousness it was so dark and I could hear people moaning and crying. I would ask for water over and over again, and speak my name and address so that someone might go and tell my parents where I was. It never occurred to me that they might have been terribly injured or killed. Then I would slip back into the beautiful place in my dreams, that glorious place.

I really do think I was dead, or very close to death. There were no doctors there, but I think if one had seen me, he would have said, "I'm sorry, but this girl is dead." I felt no pain. Just my mind was alive, in the most beautiful place I have ever seen. And I think God said, "Shigeko, this time you cannot come in. I'll wait for you the next time, but now you have to go back." It was as if I was on a mission for him. After what had happened, the bombing was followed by four days with no food or water or medical care;

with burns over a third of my body, there had to be some reason for me to have lived.

My mother had looked for me every day since the bombing. She had to walk along, turning over the bodies that looked like young girls to see if one of them was me. The fourth night my father told her not to go out anymore, but when it got late she sneaked out again to find me.

When my father and mother finally got to the auditorium they couldn't see very well because of the darkness. There were hundreds of us lying in there on the ground, most of us too badly burned to recognize. My mother screamed out my name and I answered. She told me later that it sounded like the whine of a mosquito, my voice was so soft; but, she heard it. I can still hear her voice calling me.

My face was black and my hair was black, and in the darkness my parents couldn't tell which side of my head my face was on. It was all puffed up with the burn and with infection so they couldn't see my eyes or nose or mouth, and my eyebrows and eyelashes had been burned off.

My father and another man carried me home on a wooden door. I still can feel the jolting of the door up and down and side to side. I must have been unconscious most of the time, because though it was two miles to my house it seemed like a very short trip. I was happy to be home. My body still felt numb, though, and only my mind having thoughts told me that I was alive. Every day I would pray to the stone Buddha our family had, and my mother said she was sure he heard my prayers and helped me. I lay in bed for a year. The Red Cross Hospital was not far away, but I was too sick to be carried there and the doctors were few and too busy to come to our house. I was taken care of at home, without any medicine or the help of a doctor.

All the skin around my face had to be cut and the skin peeled off so that the infection underneath could be treated. It was puffy and white and my eyes and nose and mouth were buried in it. My whole face was like raw meat that was rotting. My mother sat by my bed every day, cleaning off my face with soybean oil. I survived because my parents could take care of me. Many people died because they had no one to do that. Also, though I had been a very sickly child, I didn't get a serious illness after the bombing, even

167

though it was very unhealthy staying in the city. The water was polluted and dead bodies were rotting in the hot summer sun and there were flies everywhere. But I was healthy.

For a long time I couldn't open my mouth, my lips were turned back. I couldn't move my head because of the burned tissues in my neck. Then, gradually, my eyes could open and I could see and my nose was visible after the infection was gone. I was healing.

I have seen people die slowly. If in a bombing people die immediately, they feel no pain and have no fear, but people dying little by little is different. One of my mother's friends came over to see me while I was still bedridden. She said to my mother, "Your daughter is hurt, but you are so lucky you found her and she is alive. My daughter was under the house and half of her body was out and the other half was still buried. Nobody could help me get her out because they had problems of their own, and when the fire started people were running away and wouldn't stop. My daughter told me to go, to take her brothers and sisters and escape." The fire came closer and closer until it was burning her alive, but her mother had to leave her there. She told us she would never forgive herself for leaving her daughter there to burn to death alone, that she knew she had to save her other children, but that she should have died with her daughter. It was the most miserable kind of death. And there were many like that.

It was difficult for something like this to happen to a girl my age. Although many people, younger and older, became bitter, I was never like that. As soon as I could walk, I would go out to visit people. Yet every time I thought about how my face looked, it was hard. My parents had hidden all the mirrors in our house and so it was a year and a half before I saw it, reflected in a piece of glass I found lying on the grass. I was so scared, so shocked, I couldn't believe it was my face! I hadn't worried very much about how I looked while I was in the process of getting well, but of course I had wanted to return to living a life that was as normal as possible. At that time many people had been hurt, and so they would just look at me and say, "Oh, you were hurt, too," in a casual kind of way that didn't make me feel strange. But it became harder when the city began to be rebuilt and new people moved in from wherever they had been during the war. To these people, I

came as a shock. They would turn away their eyes from me in the street, which hurt me very much.

My two older sisters were married, and I guess I had assumed that I would just get married some day too, although I didn't think very much about it. At that time in Japan, matchmakers would introduce prospective brides to families with unmarried sons. My age was right for me to be betrothed, but the matchmakers would just look at me, say nothing, and go home. I knew, of course, it was because my face was so disfigured that they didn't want to introduce me to anybody. I had a sad, empty feeling for a while; I wasn't angry or terribly upset about it, just empty.

Then I said to myself, even if I am not given just one person to love, I can still love many people. I can love babies and old people, men and women, and it won't matter. I will love them and then they will love me. After the bombing I never went back to school, but I learned what I had to learn from observing nature. If a dog comes up to you wagging its tail, you can't kick it. You pet it. If a dog comes at you growling, you yell at it to go away and throw something at it. That is a good lesson. If I smile you will smile. If I frown you will frown. What I decided to do was to make other people happy, and if they were happy they would care for me and love me and I would be happy, too.

It was hard to do with adults at first, but it was easy with babies. I would hold them and they would smile at me. A baby doesn't smile out of politeness, he doesn't smile if he doesn't feel like it, so it was the very young who helped me first by accepting who I was beneath what I looked like. Many adults didn't want to look at me, or if they did it was with a pitying expression. Too much pity is weakening, and you don't become strong with it. With deeper people, they would smile at me even before I smiled, and that is another support I am given. And out of that kindness and caring comes peace.

Many people have said to me, "Poor you, how sad what happened to you!" But I don't feel, "poor me." It was all meant to be. God wanted me to go through everything in order to make me strong and so I could help others. If I hadn't gone through with it, I wouldn't have been strong enough and I wouldn't have appreciated human love and kindness and human life so much. Hiro-

shima came to me out of God's love, to make me strong. That's why I don't feel shy or ashamed to be out in public.

I survived to help the cause of peace. I started "Babies for Social Responsibility" to help protect babies of this world and to try to help people realize we must recognize the innocent and loving little child in ourselves and in others, to open the hearts in each other and stop war from ever happening again.

I will not think about the possibility of nuclear war and of living through that kind of bombing again. I will not permit the possibility to enter my mind. It's easy to be paralyzed by that kind of fear. Nuclear war must never happen, and so I stand here with my face to show and my experience to tell, on a mission of peace I came back from hell for.

RUTH GERNER

Ruth Gerner enlisted in the U.S. Army; as a WAVE, she coded top-secret mail headed for the Pacific Theater in World War II.

UNITED STATES

I was working in a bank in my hometown in Nevada when World War II started, and the local boys were going off to fight. We really felt the loss of all the boys because we were a ranching community and pretty soon there weren't enough kids to help run the farms. Women had to do the ranch work, then.

I enlisted in the army. I had a bad back and was panicky that they'd find out about it in the physical, and I was so happy when they didn't. I didn't feel I was cheating anyone, I just felt that once I got in I could handle any problems with my back, and contribute something. I really felt I was needed. Any girl I spoke to felt the same, all of us who enlisted when I did felt it was a patriotic move. At that time, all of us had been raised in schools that taught patriotism, so we were all flag-wavers.

I got through boot camp and then, after I was tested, they told me I could be an aviation mechanic or I could go into the medical or postal service. The only reason I chose the postal service was because I could go right in as a second class petty officer, which meant a much higher salary, at the time the grand sum of $55 a month. We had our room and board, though, and we thought it was pretty great to have all that spending money.

I was sent as a WAVE to Samson, a base camp in New York, where there were 150,000 men and 300 girls. The WAVES' barracks were surrounded by M.P.'s with guard dogs, and we couldn't go anywhere. If we wanted to buy a pair of stockings, six of us had to go together because with all the men around, they were afraid to let the girls go out alone.

I was put in charge of fifty WAVES which menat that I had to do things like make sure their hair was the right length. When it wasn't, I had to cut it because there wasn't a beauty shop on base. Some of the girls had terrible heartaches because it was their first time away from home and they were homesick; they missed their boyfriends and family.

Then I was given the choice of either going to New York or San Francisco, the only places where the Navy had fleet post offices, and I chose New York, so of course I was sent to San Francisco. It was a rough trip because of the blackouts and because men needed the trains; so we got shuttled from one troop train to another.

We worked out on Fifth and Brannan. The place was a huge warehouse with letters stacked on flats from the floor to the ceiling, from one end of the warehouse to the other. We could see right away they needed us.

Our schedule was ten hours a day, seven days a week, with the eighth day off. We worked in shifts around the clock and it still took us months just to get to the bottom of those stacks and get them sent. I worked in the Nixie Section for which we had to have special security clearance. We coded the mail to ships in the South Pacific, where fighting was going on at islands like Paleu and Truk. All of them had code names, and the ones where fighting was going on also had numbers, like 26 or 578, and no one knew what those numbers were except for us in the Nixie Section. Most of the time even the commanders on the ships didn't know where they were going. We knew before they did, and it was a very exciting part of the job that we could follow the war's progress through the numbers we had in the Nixie Section.

It was a very responsible job, and that was scary. We were warned never to go out and party too much or drink too much. We had to be a lot more careful than other people we associated with, and we were checked on all the time as to where we went and with whom. Every once in a while we'd find out our neighbors had been questioned or there was an F.B.I. check going on somewhere about you. It made me very cautious.

Of course, we also did some censoring. For the mail coming in from the South Pacific that was going to friends and family, we had to block out the names of the islands and anything that related to where they were positioned.

Sometimes I'd be sitting there, though, visualizing the Seabees attacking the enemy on the beaches, or the Marines getting off their landing craft, and all the bombing and maiming that was going on. We were very aware of the war because we saw men coming home shot to pieces, and the constant funerals and the cemeteries filling up. Sometimes the only way we could cope with what we knew was in the letters, all the personal tragedies and homesickness, was to be fully involved in the mechanics of our job, trying to remain objective and busy so the work would get done. To us the letters represented more encouragement to our men, especially the perfumed ones or those with kisses on the back. We knew that mail was the most important thing to the men during the war.

A year after I'd been there, the post office started a band. I happened to play the saxophone and thought it would be fun to give it a whirl, and we became quite good.

We happened to be playing at the Stage Door Canteen when word came that the Japanese had surrendered, and the whole place just broke loose. I couldn't believe it. They brought in a whole busload of M.P.s, Shore Patrol, to get the band members out safely. It was that bad, especially for the girls. They took us to outlying districts where we could get cabs back to our apartments, and then recommended that we lock our doors and stay there.

Next morning I learned that people had literally torn San Francisco apart! There were huge windows broken in the stores downtown, there'd been murders, there'd been rapes, people had gone just completely wild. What a way to celebrate the end of a war! It was so awful, so ugly.

After everyone else was discharged, we in the Nixie Section were frozen in our jobs, and we didn't get out until May of 1946. We had to break up the post office, particularly the politically sensitive sections, so that it could be given back to the civilians. I was a little irked at having to stay, when everyone else was getting married and going on with their lives, but I felt that I had done a very important job, and I've never been sorry I joined.

Women soldiers, embarking, World War II.

Victory march through the Arc de Triomphe, World War II.

174

Elizabeth Weidenbach, top row, second from right, in school picture, 1938.

אסתר (עלזא) בעלין, נאכ׳ן דער־
שיסן דעם ערשטן דייטש. (א בילד
פון דער סאוועטישער צפון-פראנט
צייטונג.

סתר בעלין מיט איר חבר׳טע, א סנייפערקע לידא
יאמשטשיקאווא.

Elsa Smuskevich, in sniper uniform.

Shigeku Sasamori, 1963.

Peter Forman Maker.

Connie Beedle Dixon

Evalyn Taylor.

Civil Defense Workers, World War II.

177

Hanna Voight, far right, with her family in Nazi Germany.

Esther Blanc.

Women in training, World War I.

Tsengteh Wen, far left, with her family in San Francisco, 1906.

CONNIE BEEDLE DIXON

Connie Beedle Dixon hid out with guerrillas in the Philippine jungles and fought the Japanese during World War II.

PHILIPPINES

My father was an American and my mother's family was from Spain. When they married, my mother automatically acquired American citizenship as I did when I was born. I had a sheltered childhood and though it was nice in some ways, I also did not have the freedom I wanted to have.

My ambition was to be a surgical nurse, but my parents wanted me to be a teacher, which seemed boring to me so I decided I might as well get married, instead, and have more freedom. I was wrong about that. My mother told my husband, José Vazquez, that we could live in one wing of our large house. So I was still under their noses, both in Manila and also at our summer house at Cabanatuan, where we all stayed in the summers up in the mountains where it was cooler.

Early in 1941 we knew there was going to be war. We were in Cabanatuan when Pearl Harbor was bombed and soon the Japanese started machine-gunning the town and bombing the large army base nearby. They didn't destroy our house then, but did so later on in the war. Next the occupation forces moved in and started arresting Americans and other important people, putting them in concentration camps.

In Cabanatuan a Japanese man who had owned a shoe store, and had once wanted to marry me, came to our door after the attack. He was dressed in the full uniform of a general in the Japanese army, so we guessed he might have been a spy. He told my father that he had to take us to the camp at Santo Tomàs, outside Manila, but that in two weeks he would help us to escape.

Though he told us not to take anything but necessary things with us, my mother had us hide jewelry and money on our bodies.

We went by train to Santo Tomàs, escorted by the General. I had three daughters by that time, aged four, three and one year old. We all lived in straw huts which were surrounded by a fence covered with bamboo mats. At first life there was not too bad. We had a little food and the Japanese were all right. After a few days, though, they started showing their true colors. They refused us medicine and milk for the children and were very rough on us. We were rationed maybe one cup of rice each for the whole day, and sometimes just a piece of fruit or a small fish.

All of us were scared, but at times like that you go through the motions of living, hoping for the best. You wonder when you wake up in the morning if you will see the sunset, and at night you go to sleep wondering if you will see the sunrise. This was how we were to live for the next three and a half years.

One day, we got the news that we would at last be let go, and I wrote only the date of the planned day on a piece of paper and very secretly put it through a hole in the bamboo mat where my husband was waiting for news. He had been in Manila when we were arrested and since he wasn't an American he wasn't forced to join us. But he would walk around outside the fence to get news of us, and I knew he would have a car waiting for us that day.

We received less than ten minutes' warning when it was time. We were told to make our escape as soon as possible through the side gate, to walk normally and not look back. I kept expecting every moment someone would shoot me in the back, all the time we crossed the prison yard and through the gate to the outside. My husband was parked about three blocks away and we got in the car and drove off, up to the jungle in the mountains where my father-in-law had a sugar plantation. Because it would be too dangerous for the Vazquez family, we stayed there in the hacienda for only a few days. Then we had to go into the jungle, where we built a small hut. Some friends of my father who had become guerrillas after the invasion joined us, bringing weapons. They gave me a gun, a .38 I kept strapped between my breasts at all times. Through these guerrillas we heard what was going on. Another group of guerrillas, called Hukbalahaps, were also Philippinos but they sided with the Japanese and were our enemy

also. It was difficult to tell our guerrillas from the Hukbalahaps, but there were sounds you could make, secret sounds, to identify which were our friends and which the enemy. You could whistle like a bird or make a sound like a cricket. Sometimes the only way you could tell if they were the enemy was if they had their guns up or had them pointing at you. If they were up, you were safe.

In the jungle there were deadly snakes and spiders and scorpions. There were centipedes a foot long that could kill you. Once in the jungle a troop of Japanese soldiers was passing by and we had to take cover in a ditch. While I was crouched there I heard a little rustling noise and a boa constrictor came from behind me, over my shoulder and across my chest. I was so frightened, I was more petrified than a tree that had been stone for a thousand years!

Every day we were scared. To make one move, to walk any distance, you lived in constant fear that any moment you could be shot by Japanese snipers.

We had plenty of rice in the jungle, supplied to us by the guerrillas. It was hard for the guerrillas to get us more food because they might give our location away to the enemy. We moved frequently so that wouldn't happen, but still we could not take too many risks. We had some water buffalo milk, but very little. We had plenty of fruit in season, too, but it was rice that was our staple food. We boiled up rice in a big pot and added salt and that would be what we would eat—rice soup. One time someone brought us a chicken. We boiled and boiled and boiled that chicken in a big pot with lots of water. The children ate first, and then the adults finished it up. I think it was the best meal of my life, it tasted so good!

Every third or fourth day my father would go down out of the hills to listen for news on a shortwave radio he had hidden. We had a twelve-year-old boy we called Bullet who passed on messages for us. Bullet's family had been killed; he had to stand with his father and watch his mother and sister being raped by Japanese before they were shot. Bullet had been shot in the foot, but he managed to escape and run away. My father became like a second father to him. Bullet would take the train to Manila and then sneak the news we had heard to the prisoners in Santo Tomàs by passing notes through the holes in the bamboo mats. This let the

prisoners know what was going on in the war. Then one day when Bullet was about to catch a train to Manila, he was captured and tortured terribly, but he wouldn't tell where we were, so they killed him. His death was a terrible thing, something I have not gotten over to this day.

There was an army camp outside Cabanatuan, where there were American prisoners. Once a month the Japanese allowed people to bring them food because they were starving; so if there were no enemy troops in the area, the women from our camp would take bananas and other fruit to them. Since I was lighter-skinned than the other women, and had green eyes, I had to put mud on my face and keep my eyes down if we met anyone. We would walk two days, day and night, through the jungle to the camp. There the Japanese guards would let us throw the food to where the prisoners were kept behind bars. It was so sad to see the skinny arms reaching out for the food, and to know they were so hungry. I cannot tell you how much hatred I felt then to see these people just skin and bone. I wanted to kill the whole Japanese Empire.

My friend the Japanese General had given me a pass before I left Santo Tomàs, saying that I was a good citizen and not to be molested. Though I kept it with me at all times, I didn't want to risk showing it to the Japanese because they might not believe what it said. However, I always had it with me, just in case.

My daughter got sick with a fever and we left the jungle and went down to the Vazquez' plantation. There was a woman doctor in Jaen and we could get a little medicine from her. The Japanese must have heard from the Hukbalahaps that we were there because one day, while we were sitting upstairs and talking, we suddenly heard the sound of machine-gun fire and the sound of screams and breaking windows. Quietly, without alerting the runners that were always posted on the plantation, Japanese soldiers and Hukbalahaps had surrounded the hacienda, which had already been sandbagged for protection. I told the servants that in the event we were captured, they were first to shoot my children and then shoot themselves. We all had that in our minds because being captured by the Japanese meant facing torture and a slow, terrible death.

As soon as we got downstairs I pulled the gun from my blouse and started firing through the window and over a low cement

wall. I felt no fear and had no hesitation. Being under attack and fighting, all I thought about was survival and protecting my children, as well as killing the enemy I hated so much.

For three days and two nights we fought constantly, and some of our servants and farmers, the *hacenderos*, were killed. Then the guerrillas came and encircled the enemy and saved us.

After the fight, we went back to the jungle, riding water buffaloes part of the way, and then walking. I started feeling like a murderer. I thought about the men I had killed and about their families, and I felt bad. I had never even been able to cut off the head of a chicken, and here I had killed other human beings. But then, as time went on, and we were attacked twice more, the hate and the anger grew inside me again, and with it the desire to kill.

In August of 1943, I went to Manila with my husband to give birth to my son. Although my family, the Beedles, were in danger, my husband's family was not. Besides, they were needed by the Japanese because they could supply sugar for their troops. Still it was dangerous because of my family, so we had to be very careful. There was a small hospital owned by a friend of my father's, and I had my baby there a week after I arrived. Then, when my son was five days old, my husband and I returned to the jungle, to the way we had been living.

The hardest part was watching my children go hungry. That hurt so very much. Finally I couldn't stand it any more and decided to go to Jaen and buy food. It was about a day and a half walk, and I went with a couple of women in our camp, dressed dirty and with mud in our hair to look unattractive.

During the war, most of the people who travelled around were women, because all the able-bodied men could be taken by the Japanese and conscripted by force into their army. So women did most of the work during the war. Of course it was also dangerous for women, because, for instance, the Hukbalahaps could simply say, "She's a spy," and the woman would be shot right there on the spot, no questions asked. But we had to take our chances. There was no choice. If you just sat and did nothing you might as well just shoot your brains out and have done with it all.

When we got to the marketplace, a guard said "Halt!" One Japanese soldier started kicking our legs, hard. He hit me with his gun, knocking me to the ground, and kept on kicking me. My

mouth was bloody and my eyes were blackened and two ribs were cracked. Finally an officer saw what was happening and ordered the men to leave us alone. I could barely move, so I just motioned toward my blouse. One of the women knew what I meant and pulled out the pass the Japanese General had given me. She showed it to the officer, who told the women to take me to the doctor. But I insisted we buy the food first and then, on the way out of town, stop by the doctor, because I was determined to get what I wanted for my children.

The doctor couldn't do anything for my loose teeth, and she could only bind up my chest with strips of flour sacks to help my cracked ribs. We had to walk home, but about halfway there we ran into a group of guerrillas who made a litter and carried me the rest of the way. I was so happy the children were happy. They had meat and eggs, which we had brought so carefully, carrying each egg like it was gold.

Once much later, when we women went down to town for supplies, some Japanese soldiers got all the women there together at gunpoint and divided us by age group into pens of barbed wire. Women over forty were let go. They told us then that we were to be given to the Japanese officers who were due to arrive later that day. First we would be raped by the officers, and then by the soldiers afterwards. After being raped, we knew we would be killed, so we decided we would kill the men while they were raping us, which would not be so hard to do. If we had to die, then we would take someone with us.

We waited all that day and part of the next for the officers to arrive, but they never did. They had gotten ambushed by the guerrillas, so we were let go. We returned to the jungle where we were safer, but not safe. When my children saw bodies hanging from trees with their tongues cut out, or bodies chopped to pieces or floating headless in the river, they would come running back to camp and ask me why the Japanese had killed those people. What was the answer to that? What was I to say?

Finally we heard that the Americans had landed and that the 1st Calvalry was on its way down in our direction. Soon we left the jungle for good. At the hacienda we could hear the trucks of the enemy heading towards Manila, and the sounds of gunfire and bombing. But we thought we could now celebrate liberation and

buy some food and badly needed medicine. While we were shopping, Japanese soldiers crossed the river and came into town and rounded up everyone in the village at gunpoint. They lined us all up, young and old, everyone, along the edge of a precipice.

I was sure that this was the end. They faced us with their machine guns and I prayed, "Please God, let death be instantaneous for the children." I held my son tight in my arms and heard my mother muttering insults under her breath, cursing the enemy. It is true that your life passes through your mind. In a second, a flash, from my childhood to the present moment, my whole life went past me. Then I prayed for us all to die quickly.

What happened next is why I believe in God and miracles. U.S. Navy patrol planes flew overhead, and they must have seen what was going on because they dove down lower and began to machine-gun the Japanese. We threw ourselves to the ground, and all of us were whispering, "Kill them! Kill those sons-of-bitches!" all the time the guns were firing. One plane was shot down, and I felt so sad and so angry that someone who had saved us had to die, that someone I didn't know and who didn't know us had given his life to save our lives.

After the war my children had terrible nightmares. Later they chose to forget. They've never wanted me to talk about it and I never have with them. But one day I was writing down some notes for a talk I was going to give, and my son saw that I had written about standing on the precipice with the Japanese soldiers ready to shoot us, and he said, "Mom, I remember that. That's the only part of the war that I remember." I couldn't believe it! Though he had been only a baby in my arms, he had seen what was happening and, many years later, remembered it. I remember those times, too, and the memories hurt. Though it happened over forty years ago, they will be part of me all the rest of my life. To this day I think about the men I killed. Sometimes I think that it was fine I killed them, and sometimes I feel like I am a murderer and pray God to forgive me even if I can never forgive myself. At those times I console myself and say, "That's war."

What happened all those years ago changed my outlook on life. But the good part of it is that now I open my eyes every morning with a new awareness of being alive, and I deeply appreciate everyone and everything around me.

EVE EDWARDS

Eve Edwards was evacuated from England at the age of seven and sent to Canada to live with strangers during World War II.

ENGLAND

Even though Dad was a minister and we didn't have much money, our home was very comfortable. There was lots of good food, warm fireplaces and cups of tea, and lots of hard work. There were two boys, my dad, and my mother who was pregnant; and I was about seven when we received the news that France had just been invaded. From then on I felt a strain that has never left me. My childhood was over. I did everything with the fear of bombs and of physical danger. There was that fear of not knowing and, because I was a child, not ever being told.

My father said, "We can't have the children here on the coast because the Germans are going to come right over the channel." First my brothers were sent to Scotland because we had relatives up there. Then my parents told me that I had to go away because a war was coming, and I remember thinking, "Why me?" My other friends weren't going.

Suddenly we were packing our bags. I couldn't tell my best friend I was leaving tomorrow. I did tell one child and I felt so guilty about it, I was sure we were going to get torpedoed!

The people who stayed behind drew together, determined to beat Hitler, and their effort was tremendous. I wish I could've shared in that. Instead, I had almost no way of knowing for five years if my parents were alive or dead. My brothers were sent from Scotland to Canada, but their ship was torpedoed and taken back to England. As a result, I was the only child away from my family.

I can remember seeing my mother at the station when I left; she looked as hard as nails. My dad took me down to where the boat

left from. Suddenly I was with a bunch of children; we were all bundled up together and shipped out, total strangers. And then it was the high seas, a two week haul. It was devastating, facing the unknown. All I can remember of that long trip is darkness. When I was lying in bed, the motion would make the bed go up and down. I remember the smells, I don't remember any of the people.

We got off the boat in Halifax, and then took a train to the town where I'd be staying. I lived for five years with a couple who had a daughter ten years older than me. He was a school principal and his wife, "Aunt" Lorna, was a rigid religious fanatic who had me in her home as her "war guest."

Letters were few and far between. I knew my family was being bombed and I didn't know they were alive or dead from one moment to the next. I used to get on street corners and find myself looking for my mother.

It was part of the contract that if my parents were killed in the war, and there was every chance they could be, then "Aunt" Lorna and her husband would get me, and that was the biggest worry of my life. Every day when I woke up, every night when I went to bed, I thought about going home. I guess it's like being in jail and thinking every day about when you're going to get out, and that keeps you going.

In 1945, the war was not over, but it was beginning to end and I was put on a boat and shipped home. England looked so bleak. The train station back home was bombed out completely. The middle of town was too. Houses were gone, schools were gone ... just five years later!

There was a party at home for me, and a cake with a ship on it, and there was this beautiful baby, five years old and curly-haired, this sister I'd never seen. Oh, I was so skinny and homely, with feet so big! My brothers were grand and all grown up. I was the ugly duckling, weird and odd. We never really were together again. I had a funny accent—I was Canadian—and I really felt as if I were a stranger interrupting this family's life. I didn't seem to belong to them anymore.

I felt so friendless. There was no cohesiveness between my life before and my life after the war. My school was wiped out; several of my friends had been killed and others had gone away. There was never any awareness about my alienation. Maybe that's why

I've always felt rather rootless. In some ways I would rather have had a physical disability than have something almost inexplicable. It's easier to cope with a reality than just a vague feeling of anger or anxiety or unhappiness that you have to keep inside.

I never talk about this to anyone. It doesn't seem to be worthy of any real sympathy when you think of people like the children who went to concentration camps or men who have fought in wars. I don't feel that I have the right to talk about what happened to me.

MEI NAKANO

Mei Nakano, a Japanese-American about to graduate from a Los Angeles high school, was interned in Colorado detention camps during World War II.

UNITED STATES

My parents came to this country, like many Asians, because America seemed to offer the possibility of making more money than they would have in Japan. Most of them planned to return to Japan, but when they had children, they knew to take them back to Japan would be to put them into a foreign country. My parents never had enough money to return to Japan with eight children.

They were farmers but were not typical, as they were literate and wrote for Japanese-language newspapers about their experiences in America. They wrote poetry, short stories, literary criticism, and essays about the unfair treatment not only of the Japanese, but also of the Mexicans and Blacks. My parents felt this discrimination very clearly, especially since there was the Alien Land Law at that time which denied my father, who was a very capable and scientific farmer, the right to buy land; he had to remain a sharecropper. You couldn't become a naturalized citizen of the United States until 1954, and before that there was this catch-22 situation where you couldn't buy land unless you were a citizen, but you couldn't become a citizen if you were Asian.

My father told us as we grew up that we were to study hard and grow up to be good Americans; but, on the other hand, he would tell us that we were Japanese and should learn our own culture and language.

When I was young I wanted more than anything else to be American. I used to look at myself in the mirror and feel I was cursed with the very Japanese-looking face. I felt I was often ridi-

culed for acting foolish, and I always felt it was because I was different, I was Japanese. However, I was shrewd enough to know it was important to be pleasing and to do certain things in society. I always knew how to get along in the world.

There were a lot of rumors before World War II started. Quite some time before the war, our travel was curtailed to a five-mile radius from home, and there was an order that we always carry our identification cards with us, which made us feel awful. There was so much inflammatory material in the newspapers that the climate in Los Angeles was one of terrible hate and prejudice. Finally, we didn't have any good friends who weren't Japanese.

There were places we could go and places we couldn't. Going to school in the streetcar, sometimes people would very obviously turn away or keep me from sitting next to them, and it was excruciating. One becomes very sensitive to that kind of rejection, and I don't think that sensitivity has ever left me.

We lived in Los Angeles for five years when the war broke out in December, 1941. By then my father had died at fifty of heart problems. My mother was too proud to go to the government for charity, but she accepted the handouts of churches and people who knew us.

I was supposed to be graduated from high school in June of 1942, but I had to quit in May because we were evacuated to internment camps and my mother had no one at home to help her to prepare.

We weren't allowed to have shiny things, like mirrors or knives, because the government thought we might try to send signals to the enemy. They told us to bring our bedding and clothing, and that was all. Waves of people came through our neighborhoods, buying cheaply all the things we would have to leave behind.

There were signs posted on the telephone poles in Japanese neighborhoods listing where we would have to gather on the day of deportation. An area had been roped off in the street, and outside the rope were spectators or friends of those who were going. There were soldiers with guns and bayonets standing around guarding us, but there wasn't any trouble.

The soldiers directed us onto trucks. Since Japanese people tend to be very cognizant of the needs of other people, everybody was

too concerned about one another's comfort and behaving in an orderly fashion to be causing trouble with the soldiers. The dominant feeling was that we had to take care of each other, that our survival was somehow based on a feeling of cooperation.

From the truck we were transported to Santa Anita Racetrack, which was being used as an "assembly center," and we spent the months from May to September there. It was very hot. Some of the people stayed in horse stalls and some of us in hastily-erected barracks which were all lined outside with black tar paper, which absorbed all the heat.

One of the big problems was that many of us got dysentery and we had to wait in long lines to try to get to a toilet. Very often you couldn't make it, which was terribly embarrassing. We never showed ourselves naked in front of anybody, but suddenly there were only these open showers and open toilets in a row, and we'd all wash at a common basin.

Five months later we were uprooted and sent to a relocation center in a flat and treeless part of Colorado. The camp was surrounded by barbed wire. There were row after row of barracks divided into blocks, like separate communities, with each block having its own washroom, toilets (where we put up curtains to provide some amount of personal privacy), a mess hall, and a recreation room that had two Ping-Pong tables where we could have dances and hang our laundry out in the winter. Each "apartment" was only one room with a potbellied stove and a doorless cupboard, its size in accordance with the size of the family occupying it.

The camp became a self-contained community, with a school and a co-op we started. Very quickly we tried to develop some kind of working life. Where there was a father in the family, it was apparently very difficult for him because he was no longer the breadwinner. His children could also work and he didn't need to do anything if he didn't want to. A lot of fathers started drinking.

I got a job teaching kindergarten. I was on the lowest pay scale because I had only a high school education, and got paid $8.00 a month for working eight hours a day, five days a week.

Many families suffered disintegration. It was a great loss to us because traditionally, Japanese families tend to be close-knit. My older brothers, who were helped by the Quakers to go to a Chris-

tian college in New York, were not allowed to come back to the coast.

When I was seventeen, I had met my husband-to-be on a blind date, and then I found him again in camp. We started spending a lot of time together. We were married on Easter Sunday in a converted barracks, the first wedding in camp. I probably wouldn't have married him if we hadn't been in camp together and I hadn't been so insecure about myself. I needed his steadiness and his strength. Though I wasn't terribly conscious of it at the time, I had no sense of the future. What I could see ahead for myself was only my death, about which I didn't feel fear, just a kind of hopelessness. What I wanted most was to experience myself as a woman, and have a child. I didn't think about my child's future, just myself and my needs. I felt my husband and I were both going to die, that we would never get out of camp alive, and I wanted to have a child that would be part of us both.

When my son, Chris, was born he had a severe case of diarrhea, which was probably due to my poor nutrition. I wasn't informed that I should eat more healthfully because I was pregnant. I was just supposed to show up in time for the delivery. Soon after Chris was born he got jaundice. I felt if he died it would be the end of me, but he came through it. By the time he was three months old, and very sickly, my husband was drafted. He was assigned to Army Intelligence because, the army figured, since he'd had some education in Japan and could speak both languages well, he'd be a good person to interpret messages for them.

I felt very sorry for myself, and I knew I was going to be very lonely. I didn't think about how unfair it was that the government would first put him in an internment camp and then draft him, that's how limited my thinking was!

When my son was eleven months old we rejoined my husband who had been sent to Minnesota. We travelled by train. I felt everyone on the train must surely be able to see how tainted I was: a non-American. I had the lowest self-image that I ever had in my life.

I had another child in Minnesota, and then my husband got orders to go overseas. I went to live in Chicago where my family had relocated. Racial prejudice in the Midwest wasn't nearly what it had been in Los Angeles.

The war was over by the time my husband came home, and my family and I had moved from Chicago back to Los Angeles. California didn't want the Japanese to relocate in the state because it was "too dangerous." We felt very much like unwanted guests and tried to behave well and be exemplary citizens. I remember feeling that I wanted to be as invisible as possible and not do anything which would make me stand out.

After the war there were many proscriptions about where certain races, including the Japanese, could buy homes or property. My husband and I decided we would not buy a house in a ghetto. We were determined to buy a house where we wanted our children to be raised, in a neighborhood we liked. Although there was some initial trouble, things calmed down and the neighbors accepted us.

I wanted our children to have everything I didn't have. I wanted our children to be bona fide citizens in this country. I wanted them to have friends who would respect them and not say, "You're my friend at school but not outside of school," as it had been for me.

Our older two children are now married to white people and our youngest says he won't marry, but all of them have mostly white friends. We had wanted them to integrate into society, and we did our job almost too well; now they are so American they are disconnected from Japanese culture.

Things have changed, and yet there is still a lot of prejudice against Asian-Americans—we are all lumped together whether we're Japanese, Chinese, Vietnamese or whatever. It would be foolish, possibly dangerous, to ever forget what we experienced in World War II. That kind of injustice could happen again.

EVALYN TAYLOR

Evalyn Taylor worked in the San Francisco shipyards during World War II painting and repairing battleships.

UNITED STATES

On December 7, 1941, I was living in San Francisco with my ten-year-old son and my husband, who worked in the shipyards as a painter. When the war began, my husband had to work day and night and I really wanted to help the war effort. I decided to get a job in the shipyards. At that time, I actually don't think I liked being a woman very much, and I think I had to get to know the masculine part of myself before I could accept the feminine part. My work in the shipyards was a way to come together.

About this time, my husband decided he would like to join the Merchant Marine. I took his place in the shipyards as a painter, and because he had been president of the painters' union, I was acceptable to them, and was elected to an office.

Masses of people were employed there, just like a city, and when the shifts would change I felt a part of all humanity. I was drinking pretty heavily, and would leave the shipyard at noon to get a beer and a double shot of whiskey and get a little bottle filled up to take back to work with me. A lot of people did that, of course. It was just the common workingman's life, and I really enjoyed it. I felt I was really living. Why I didn't become an alcoholic, I don't know. Many members of my family were. I think work stopped me, because if I took on a job it was important to me to do it well.

At first some of the men made passes at me to see what I would do, but as soon as they saw I wasn't having any of that, I didn't have any more trouble. When they saw I really could do the work they respected me. They didn't know what to do with us women and were a little bit leery of us working alongside them, wondering if we could take the rough language, which was pretty funny.

There was a lot of ridicule of the women in the shipyards, a lot of sexual jokes, but then there were some women who plied a different trade than what they were originally hired to do! I wore coveralls and a bandana around my head, and I decided either I could do the real work of the shipyard or I wasn't going to stick around. I had to feel productive.

You got paid $1.20 an hour on new work, shellacking woodwork and so forth, work that Bethlehem Steel had contracted. The government paid you for repair work on damaged cruisers and destroyers—and they paid $1.49. After a while only two female painters were put on repair work, and I was one of them. You could get away with a lot because the government paid you if you worked or not, and there wasn't any pressure put on you to work very hard, but sitting around drove me crazy. Bethlehem Steel hired anybody—no matter how many people were put on a job— just because the government paid for them. It didn't really matter whether they were used or not. This corruption disillusioned people who wanted to feel they were helping in the war.

For example, one of the first jobs I was assigned was to camouflage a ship. They snap chalklines with a string all over the ship's exterior, and then mark initials down on the sections for whatever colors they're to be painted. I worked on the gun turret, painting it with one color and then another, and I don't know how long it took me to get all that tedious work done, but as soon as I'd finished the order came down, "Paint it 'battleship gray'!"

They gave women the lousiest jobs. We'd have to mask off areas that were not to be painted, then the spray painters would come by, and then afterwards we'd have to strip all the masking tape off. The spray painters, who were men, got a higher wage, and so did the men who did much the same work as women did.

It was very hard work but, you see, the Lord prepared me for it because I used to milk cows on the farm growing up, and had very strong hands! I liked hard work, but sometimes the physical strain wasn't nearly as hard as the emotional. One time a destroyer was laid up in dry dock while we were getting it ready to go out. We got to know all the sailors because they were living on board while we were working. We'd loan them money so they could go see their girlfriends, and they'd tell us about their families. Finally the ship was repaired and ready to leave. We all stood on the dock

and waved them goodbye. It couldn't have been a month before the ship came back crippled. A Japanese suicide bomber had gone down one of its stacks. When the ship came in with the survivors, we went out on the dock to welcome them home.

All these young men were just standing there, looking at us, through us, and beyond us. I had an awful, sick feeling because I knew that somehow they couldn't talk to us anymore; they couldn't share with us what had happened because they had known a hell that we didn't know.

The war went on and I started to have trouble with the painters' union because there were some questionable payments being made and some funny business was going on with the union funds. The International wanted to close down the painters' union and take it over. We were going to have a meeting about it one night, and I was in a bar having a drink before it started when the goon squad came in and surrounded me and said something about shaping up and shutting up. I went to the meeting anyway, but I was scared. It was finally a court decision whether or not the International could close the painters' union down. It didn't take me long to discover, however, after our union was taken over, that the International was just as corrupt as the painters' union had been, and I didn't have anything more to do with any of them.

Roosevelt's death was really more powerful, I think, than either V-J or V-E Day. It was midafternoon and the rumor started going around that Roosevelt was dead. I was on the day shift, and there was a light drizzle, I remember, as we left work. Usually when the shifts changed there'd be a rush of people going in and out and the noise and clamor would be deafening. But on this day no one made a sound. You could only hear the slight shuffling of feet and the cry of the newsboy, "Roosevelt is dead!" People were stunned, and I think the heart went out of us at that point, although after that came the surge of wanting to do what we were doing in his memory. He was so greatly loved! The first time I ever voted, I voted for him.

I was with the all-woman crew when we got the news the war was over. We just picked up and left because we knew there'd be no more work for us. I went immediately to my apartment, locked the door and didn't answer the telephone. I didn't want to be part of that absolute madness. It was a crazy time: people were killed,

197

trampled, they jumped out of windows. I had sensed that hysteria was going to take place and I was terrified of the irrational feeling of it. I just wanted to curl up in a hole and wait it out.

It made me sad that victory was being celebrated that way when we had paid such a high price in the war; and I was also sad because I knew it was an end to something else. I had to face a lot of changes in my own life.

My husband Jimmy had become an alcoholic. I decided to move up to Reno to live with a friend. I lived there for a year, but I couldn't forget Jimmy and I had a very strong need to go back and see how he was. But I couldn't find him. I went back to Reno where I was working as a waitress and a painter and in a short time I got a letter from his sister back in Kansas saying that Jimmy had died. He'd been on board ship, and he and some other men were below deck having a drink to celebrate their signing on. There were three whiskey bottles on a shelf in the engine room and Jimmy grabbed one and took a big slug. It was carbon tetrachloride. The engineer had put it into a whiskey bottle to have it handy when he needed to clean the engines.

I almost went out of my mind when I got that letter. His loss hurts me to this day. If I hadn't worked and found the confidence I needed in myself, I might not have been able to survive his death. But I had learned that I could take care of myself. I think my shipyard experience helped me to accept who I am and to get to know more about myself through the interaction with so many people. I developed a sense of the masculine qualities and strengths I have, and I felt a confidence I had never felt before. I felt a real joy in making my way in a man's world.

My husband left me a small insurance policy, enough for me to get my teeth fixed and go back to high school. I supported myself and my son as a waitress and painter. The insurance money got me started on a new life, so my husband is really a part of all I have now, all that I have become.

I don't look back very often, mainly because the past is part of me. The war was not outside of me because I was in it and I needed some distance to see it whole. Now in my life I feel a sense of completion and a sense of who I am. The threads of my life are all coming together, and the fabric is strong.

ESTHER BLANC

Esther Blanc, a nurse from Goshen County, Wyoming, volunteered in the fight against fascism in Spain in 1936; she tended the wounded in front-line hospitals.

SPAIN

My mother and father went to Wyoming on a homesteading experiment with a colony of other Jews. They believed in American idealism and the ethics of the frontier. I was born in their sod house in 1913, one of six children who survived.

My parents took the *Daily Forward*, a Jewish, left-of-center newspaper delivered everyday by the rural mail delivery. Mother would read it to us and we would discuss what she read. My parents had left Rumania to get away from a society which was fiercely inequitable. They really believed America was the land of opportunity, land of the free, and they instilled this feeling in us.

One thing one had to learn growing up in Goshen County, Wyoming, was how to think. Once you left the farm and its outbuildings, you were on your own. That gave me a scientific attitude, which in turn helped me to be a very good clinician. I had wanted to be a physician. I loved surgery. But my family was poor and couldn't afford to send me to college, so I became a nurse instead. At first I earned my living doing mostly private duty; then, in 1936, I went to work for the U.S. Public Health Service at the U.S. Marine Hospital in San Francisco. The hospital atmosphere was charged because of the Spanish civil war, and patients kept maps on the walls with pins in them to chart the war's progress.

Interest in the Spanish civil war was particularly strong among those of us who were Jewish and well aware of what was happening in fascist Germany. I had met quite a few German-Jewish refugees, and had become what was known as a "premature anti-

fascist." We knew exactly why we were antifascist and the war in Spain was a very clear-cut proposition to us.

I was twenty-three when I volunteered in 1936, and I felt that I was volunteering for all the Jews all over the world and all the people who were being oppressed by the Nazis and other fascists. I could only see them as enemies of the United States because we were a democracy. I felt noble about what I was doing, and also very sympathetic for the people of Spain and what they were going through.

We were screened very thoroughly because they didn't want any adventurers or crackpots. We had an aura of great respectability under the aegis of the American Refugee Committee to Aid Spanish Democracy. There were about nineteen in our group, coming from all different areas in the United States.

We docked at Port-Bou, on the Spanish-French border, and then travelled down to Valencia, and across to the headquarters of the International Brigades, in Albacete. The Commandant of the Brigades asked my friend Irene and me if we wanted to go to the American Hospital in Huete which was overcrowded with the wounded from the Front. We worked there for a month, and then when orders came down that there was going to be an offensive on the Madrid Front, we were transferred to the 35th Division, which is where we stayed.

There were forty-eight different national groups represented, people from China and Japan and Israel and Poland and every country you ever heard of. We came from all kinds of political affiliations: Communists and Socialists and Social Democrats, as well as idealistic ladies from Wyoming, like me, who had been taught so well how to be an American that Spain was a logical place to end up. And so it was for everyone I knew who went to Spain. We had been born in ghettos of some kind and were fighting for freedom. All of us had a profound desire to preserve the rights of man.

We were a M.A.S.H. unit, although we didn't call ourselves that, a mobile unit that moved from place to place along the Front, the first Front Line hospital behind Battalion Headquarters. We were set up in local buildings as soon as the Division would be fighting nearby.

My work with casualties was painful because the injuries were so terrible, but there wasn't much time to get emotional. Exhaus-

tion was the universal feeling, I suppose. I used to get to the unit at seven in the morning and, except for lunch and supper, it would be a continual round of changing dressings until eleven o'clock at night. I must've had fifty patients in my ward, from all over the world. Though I knew Yiddish and some German, I didn't know any Spanish, but I picked it up very fast.

In its own way the war was very interesting and, I suppose, romantic. The international effort was wonderful. When the war started, the religious orders fled the Republic whenever they could because the Catholic Church was on the side of Franco and the fascists, and so we were able to use the facilities they'd abandoned. When we were on the Madrid Front, we set up a hospital down the road from Philip II's palace, the Escorial, in a convent with a lovely pear orchard.

We were often within two miles of the Front and were frequently bombed and strafed by machine-gun fire. We were in danger "something considerable," as we would say out in Wyoming. Sometimes I was truly scared out of my wits. One time travelling with a British woman journalist from Valencia to Barcelona, we came to a town that was being bombed. We waited on the outskirts until all the planes, which were many and German, left the area. The devastation was terrible. There were live electrical wires everywhere and bodies and children screaming and there was absolutely nothing we could do. Another time, we evacuated a place only a couple of hours before it was bombed and flattened to the ground.

I never felt well the whole time I was in Spain, but I endured it. I got dysentery right away; then I got malaria, but it was the undulant fever that finally did me in. Every afternoon at four o'clock I got cold chills and ran a fever that would last until ten o'clock at night. Finally, no longer useful, I had to leave. I felt terrible, as if I were letting everyone down. I knew I was needed, and there I was, laid out.

I felt much better in Paris, and then I went on to London, where I felt so much better that I entertained the hope of being able to go back to Spain. But then a malaria test showed that I had the disease in its worst form, and there was no way I could go back.

I felt awful. They shipped me out the next day. The war was still going on, it was only July of 1938, and fighting would con-

tinue for almost another year. I knew I could've done a lot more. It was terrible to listen to the news on the radio and to be able to do nothing. I felt defeated, helpless. When Madrid fell, I went into a depression which just didn't lift. I mourned for Spain and for what was going to happen to its people. I sat "Shiva," as if for a person, and grieved for Spain.

What I feared for the people did come to pass. In one instance, there was a deep chasm with a river winding through it outside of the town of Cuenca, near where I had been stationed. The fascists filled that chasm with people and then machine-gunned them to death. There must have been Cuencas throughout Spain. There were many others just shot out of hand and many sent to prison where they stayed for years and years, and were eventually executed.

After my period of mourning, I knew clearly what the world was up against, but that I was powerless to help very much. There's that old saying, "If you aren't willing to learn from the lessons of history, you will have to repeat its mistakes." A great many people in politics seem not to learn anything from history.

I learned a great deal from the war. It showed me what I was capable of doing, given a situation where I was forced to use all of my resources. Very few people get the chance to learn that, especially as young as I was. In that respect, the war altered my whole life, because it taught me how well I could perform under circumstances which were extremely difficult. It gave me a greater confidence in myself.

I think the thing that makes me different from many other members of the International Brigades is that I never look back. I don't go to meetings very often or even think about the war very much. I haven't made a career out of having been in Spain. I've had many careers since, as a genetics technician, operator of a Chinese orphanage, nurse in a polio epidemic; and then in 1944, when Roosevelt asked for all available nurses to volunteer, I went into the Army, where I worked in the isolation wards for communicable diseases, and then was briefly in the Air Corps just at the end of World War II.

I'm proud of what I did in Spain, but it is only part of what has been a very full life, a life very fully lived. The life I always wanted, and was lucky enough to have!

TSENGTEH WEN

Tsengteh Wen, a lifelong revolutionary, supported Sun Yat-sen against the Manchu Dynasty, pioneered English-language education in Mao's time, and was imprisoned by Red Guards during the 1966-1970 Cultural Revolution.

CHINA

My father came from China to San Francisco right after the Gold Rush, and he died just before I was born in 1900. My sisters and I went to a segregated school because up until college Asian children were not permitted to go to the same schools as white children. It was racial discrimination and it hurt our feelings very much to be treated as inferiors.

Then came the 1911 Revolution, initiated by Dr. Sun Yat-sen, who wanted to overthrow the Manchu Dynasty. We knew the reason we could be treated so badly in the United States was because we had a very weak government that allowed it. Even at ten years old I understood that what the revolution was doing was important for China. I knew it was to help us have a strong country and a strong government, a government that would not allow the Americans or the British to look down on us any longer.

There was a secret organization called the Tung-Meng-Hui that needed many members to help, so I joined it when I was ten years old, along with the rest of my family. We had to be very careful. We had secret signs to identify each other, such as the way we would put our spoons on top of our soup bowls, or how we would place our chopsticks on our bowls of rice when we greeted the other diners at the table in customary Chinese etiquette.

Finally Dr. Sun came to the United States on a fund-raising campaign. Because he knew we were in the Tung-Meng-Hui, he sought shelter in our house when thugs from the tongs tried to

kidnap him. The Chinese Consulate paid them to do this, both in Britain and then, later in the United States.

Dr. Sun was a very nice man, always very polite. I asked him many naive questions which he always answered very kindly. For instance, once I asked him, "How can the guns for the revolution get through customs?" He explained to me that they were smuggled into China in coffins, which was a very brave act that could cost the smugglers their lives.

The Tung-Meng-Hui expanded from a small group to a very large one when Dr. Sun visited, and we began to raise funds. When the revolution succeeded Dr. Sun went back to China to act as Provisional President. We had a big parade to celebrate. I got to ride on one of the floats, all dressed up and carrying flowers. On the side of the float it read, "Long Live the Republic! Monarchy is Dead!" I felt so proud. I felt that now I could hold up my head and never have it bowed again.

After the revolution was over there was nothing more for us to do. We just led our everyday lives until 1914. I still felt like an American citizen but was angry about the racial discrimination I suffered and did not want to attend the segregated high school the next year. I settled my mind to go live in China. There was too much injustice for me; it made me too angry, and also I wanted a good education. By then my brother had become a Senator in China, where he had gone with Dr. Sun Yat-sen, and we made up our minds to follow him.

I went back to China with my mother and my one unmarried sister on February 14, 1914. I didn't feel that I was leaving the United States forever, but as it turned out I stayed in China for the next seventy years.

Later, after I was married, people kept saying I was American, and that I even looked foreign. They would say, "But you have such a high nose!" They hadn't seen any foreign people and didn't know any better. That is what happens when you have a closed-door policy.

From 1928 to 1956, I lived in Hong Kong with my husband, where we ran a newspaper and wire service. In 1956, after the liberation of China from Chiang Kai-shek, I wrote to Chou En-lai asking if I could offer my knowledge of English to China. He wrote me back, in his own hand, "You are heartily welcome home. We can use whatever you have to offer."

I returned to China alone, leaving my husband in Hong Kong. It was easy for me to leave, really, because of the deep feeling I had for China and the strong desire to be of service. I have always had a strong will, and whatever I decided to do in my life, I have done. I realized that after the liberation everything was changed into the Soviet-style Communism and that it was important not to have a closed-door policy with the rest of the world, but to keep communication open with the English-speaking countries.

I never saw my husband again. I was not allowed to Hong Kong. I wasn't permitted an exit visa while my husband was still alive. Oh, it was painful sometimes to be away from him, especially when he would write to me about his difficulties with the newspaper now that I wasn't there to help him with it.

I met Chou En-lai in Shanghai. I told him I wanted to teach. There is a Chinese saying, "To grow a tree it takes ten years, to grow a man takes a hundred years." I wanted to teach English because I felt knowledge of that language was a tool that could make China strong in the world.

I was stationed at the Foreign Languages Institute in Shanghai. The trouble was that there were no books whatsoever in China to teach English conversation. I said, "How am I going to teach without books?" and I was told, "You'll have to write them." So I wrote the first of a series of books for all Chinese schools and universities. In fact, these were the first books on English grammar and conversation available in China.

I taught conversation until 1966, at the beginning of the Cultural Revolution, when we were all "re-educated." Chiang Ching wanted to be the Chairman of the People's Republic of China after her husband, Mao Tse-tung, was dead. The workers and farmers couldn't think much about it or be in a position to see what was going on, but the intellectuals knew. So thousands and thousands of intellectuals were killed, tortured to death.

One day the Red Guard came to my house and told me I was to go immediately to the institute. I knew I was under arrest because they told me to take my bedding, and only my bedding, with me. I think I was so overly frightened that I didn't feel anything at all.

I took my bedding and toothbrush and towel and only the light summer clothes I had on me at the time. At the institute I was put into a classroom. It was locked all the time and I was only allowed out three times a day, when I would empty the bucket I had to use

as a toilet, get fresh water for drinking and bathing, and pick up my food. I stayed there several months, and I suppose it wasn't so bad—it had a window. It was barred, however, and to look at the bars was so sad. It was terrible to see the sky through the bars, so I just stopped looking out after a while.

The Red Guard would come into the room and ask over and over again questions like why was I born in America. They told me that I was a traitor because of the fact I corresponded with relatives in the United States and that I was an intellectual. The Red Guard was critical of what I had written during the Sino-Japanese War. Even my innocent English conversation book, written carefully without slogans, was banned as a "black book," an obscene book. (Later, Deng Xiaoping had my book published and distributed.)

I was beaten every evening from eight o'clock to midnight, for two months. They beat me with a chair leg everywhere that wouldn't show. Because I didn't cry they beat me a very long time. I would not cry for mercy from them! The more they tried to make me cry the more I was determined not to. It hurt, but what I felt more than pain was outrage that I could be beaten brutally for something I did not do.

After several months they asked me a question I tried to answer but could not answer. I wrote out an answer they did not like and they gave me the heaviest punishment, imprisonment in a 3′ by 3′ cubicle, without a chair or table or bed. There was no window, either, so the room would often be like an oven in the heat.

I had to write down long answers to satisfy the unanswerable questions of the Red Guard, holding the paper on my knee and writing sometimes from dawn to dark and dark to dawn. I wasn't even given the paper, but had to buy it. I always thought, even for the nine months in the cubicle, that someday the evil of the Cultural Revolution would be over.

I feel sorry to say that I had no feelings at all, or rather tried to have no feelings, while I was in the cubicle. All I did was wait to die. There was nothing safe to think of and nothing to do but write those endless answers. The whole country was like a giant prison, and if I had managed to escape, where would I have gone? There was nothing to think about but your last moment, your death.

It was piercing to my heart to be away from my children and to

know so little about how they were doing. My daughter had been sent to the countryside to farm, where she planted seeds for two years. The farmers were kind to her. But my son had been put in a concentration camp in the country where he was systematically tortured. I was so afraid that something worse would happen to him because of me. I managed to get a letter sent to him in which I encouraged him to study mathematics, because then he wouldn't need a laboratory or any kind of equipment, things that could be taken away from him. That is what he subsequently did.

In 1968, after nine months, I was sent to the countryside to work on a farm, and I had to learn to reap the harvest. Oh, we had to bend down for so many hours! I was at the farm with several other professors, and the farmers told the Red Guard that we were too old to do such hard work. I was 72 years old, and the others were about the same. The Red Guard thought we had asked the farmers to appeal for mercy, so they made us pick stones out of the fields.

The farmers were so kind to us. For instance, they knew we were often hungry, and so when they had some nice piece of meat they would wrap it up in a piece of cloth, because paper would have crackled when it was opened and given us away, and they would place it silently beneath our pillows and go quietly away. I think of them often with love.

I was finally released in 1970 to write conversational material for the Red Guard. I was still watched continually and kept locked in my room. We had to study all the time, editorials and so forth, and then we had to discuss them in a group. This they called "rehabilitation." I was smarter by this time and just went along with everything.

When they felt I had been re-educated, they released me to my own home to write conversational material. I was still under surveillance. It was so uncomfortable to be watched all the time, but most of the time I just felt their presence, their eyes on me. I didn't go out or visit anyone. I would go to work at school early and return home late. They called teachers like us "monsters," and we weren't allowed to teach; but I did continue to write conversational material all day, then go home at night to write out for the Red Guard all the information about my day. I knew my neighbors also watched me, watched the lights go on and off in my house, so I was careful not to be too long in the bathroom, for instance, so they wouldn't wonder what I was up to. It was impor-

tant to the Red Guard to know everything about you—that was the way they were able to read your mind.

I tried not to think too much about my children, only that I had to remain vigilant and not make a mistake that would make their lives worse.

Then Mao passed away and Deng Xiaoping overthrew Madame Mao and the Gang of Four two years after I was finally released from suspicion, in 1974. A document was issued that said the Cultural Revolution had come to an end and what had happened since 1967 was wrong, that we would no longer be called "rightists" and would have our freedom.

The Communist Party at the institute held a meeting and announced that I had been wrongly treated during the Cultural Revolution. I had no feeling of joy. I knew I had done nothing wrong! Because of the years I spent working for Dr. Sun Yat-sen in the United States, as well as my experiences writing political articles for our newspaper in Hong Kong, I became valuable to the government. In 1978, I was asked to become a member of the People's Consultative Committee, a group of intellectuals who discuss problems in the country. I like helping in the P.P.C.C., particularly in what I can do for ordinary people who come to ask for my help. I still feel I have much to learn. I want to continue teaching for as long as I live, both because I must have something to do and because teaching is such a pleasure to me. When I teach my people to speak English I hope they will be able to do something for China, that the knowledge of other languages will make China stronger. I have taught doctors and scientists and exchange students who have gone west to study and then bring their knowledge home. That is very fulfilling to me!

Whether you are an intellectual or a housewife or a farmer, everybody in China respects what everyone else does. It is everyone's duty to contribute. One's daughter and son have a duty to their country just as they do to their family, but now that I am old I think first of my country and second of my family. Of course, I suppose that has always been true, in a way. If I had not felt that, I would not have left my husband to die alone in Hong Kong when I returned to China.

My feeling during the years of my imprisonment was that I was in a long nighttime, and even if I never woke to see it, night becomes dawn and dawn leads to day. Daylight would sometime be, and China would be strong.

Violet Pasdermajian Goliti was driven into exile from Erzerum in 1915, the last year of a systematic plan for the extermination of the Armenian people by the Turkish regime of Abd al-Hamid II.

ARMENIA • TURKEY

I was born in Erzerum, Turkish Armenia, in 1902. My father was very rich, the director of a large bank, and we had a nice life. We owned lots of land and a flour mill and we had thirty-four families working for us. There was a mosque in our city, with a bell tower as big as a church, that my grandfather had built. He and my grandmother were buried in it.

Armenia was surrounded in the beginning by Turks, Russians and Persians, and Armenia got divided between them, with no safe place for Armenians to live. Turks had always been our enemies, but we couldn't do anything against them since this was our home and we had somehow to live together in peace. Turks are lazy and Armenians are very .hardworking, so we had more than the Turks had. I think jealousy made the Turks do what they did to us. There had always been trouble with them before the exile, but adults didn't talk in front of us children about it. Still, I remember waking from nightmares about being chased and hurt by Turkish boys who used to threaten us after school. It was an uneasy peace, and even children must have felt the danger and hostility under the surface of everyday life.

One day, when my father was due to come home from the bank, someone came and pounded on our door. Our servants ran out and then came back to tell us that someone had shot my father, but that the Turks wouldn't let his body be brought home until they were sure he was dead. It was wintertime and his body lay in the snow with knife wounds in his sides and a bullet in his head.

We never knew who killed him, except that they were Turks.

I remember that day very well. It is burned in my memory like fire. I thought it was the end of my life. My mother had died just two months before in childbirth because her doctor had been sent off to war and she couldn't get the right medical help. My older brothers who were in school in Constantinople were killed by the Turks, too, at about this same time.

The exile started in 1915. I was thirteen and had two younger brothers and an older sister. The Turks didn't exile all the Armenians in the city at the same time; we were divided into groups, and our group was the last to leave. At first, because my father was dead and families without men were not supposed to be exiled, we thought we might be able to stay in our home. But finally they made us go, too.

German soldiers helped the Turks do this to us. We had lots of dogs in the streets in Erzerum, and the Germans had said, "Clean up those dogs from the streets." The Turks went out and killed the dogs, and the Germans said, "We didn't mean those dogs, we meant the Armenians." Later, when Hitler was asked how he thought he could get away with killing so many Jews, he said, "Who remembers the Armenians?"

One night Turkish soldiers came to our house and told us we had to get out of our house and out of the city. At first we all thought we could return home after the war, so we stored our belongings in the church for when we returned. Most of our jewelery was in the bank, with bonds and money, and all of it was stolen after we left.

The next night, when the Turkish soldiers came back, they told us to get out of our house and they forced us into their carriages. We brought as much gold as we could, but nothing else. The soldiers drove us outside the city walls, dropped us off, and then locked the gates behind us. We walked to the next town and bought carriages and big tents and portable beds and trunks full of food. We even had champagne to drink along the way. Then the soldiers who were supposed to march us into exile told us that we would be climbing mountains and could only use donkeys and mules, so we had to leave most of our things behind. We gave the champagne to the soldiers so they would take good care of us, but they didn't.

We rented seven very expensive mules in town, but when we got to the place where we were going to start off the next day, we found that the men who had rented us the mules had thrown all of our belongings on the ground, had taken the mules and our money, and had disappeared. There was only one mule left to buy, so we would only take the most essential things.

For the next several months we just walked. Every night we slept outside, and the next morning we had to continue on when the soldiers told us to. Sometimes we had to walk across such narrow places in the mountains that some of the people fell over the cliffs. Anyone who got sick was thrown in the river to drown. I was sick, and it was difficult to walk, but my sister used to say, "Get up and walk or they'll throw you in the river!"

I don't know how many in our group were killed along the way, because other groups from other cities joined us as we went along, but I do know that out of my big family only one aunt, a cousin, my two brothers and sister survived. Many, many people died. One day the soldiers said to us that they were going to take all the men and older boys to a place where they could buy or build some houses, where we could all live, but they took them away and killed them somewhere in the mountains. Then they took the young boys and girls and women to a building on a mountainside, and we all had to be searched to see if we had any money. We had heard what they were going to do from some other people who had already been searched, so we put our gold coins in a water container and the Turks didn't think to look in there. That's how we saved some money to buy bread along the way, and that is how we survived.

Oh, we walked and walked! Along the way there were so many bodies in the river, and where the water was shallow their hair floated on the water. We could smell the stink of rotting bodies along the way. Later, when we had nothing to drink and the rivers were dry, we had to dig in the sand for water near where putrified bodies were lying. It was horrible, but we were so thirsty even that couldn't stop us from trying to get a mouthful of water.

Every day was very dangerous for us. We prayed never to be walking last in line because Turks on horseback would come and take you away. They would come riding out from behind trees in the forest, and if they could, they would grab you up and ride

away with you. I had nightmares for most of my life about them. Turks liked to have the women and girls they stole to rape or to become their wives. Many girls, when they saw the Turks coming on their horses, would hold each other's hands and throw themselves over the cliffs into the rivers and drown.

I saw so many bodies! The Turks often did terrible things to the people they killed. One man hid under a dead body and later got away and returned to us. The Turks had cut off his nose, and had done many other things like that to the others, he told us. There were hills of bodies and hills of cut-off heads. I cannot tell you of the horror!

My cousin was pregnant when we left Erzerum, and along the way she had her baby. She couldn't take care of it, she had no milk, so she wrapped it up in a piece of her clothing and left it under a tree near a village of Kurds. A lady saw her do this, and she took my cousin's baby home. Later, one of my cousin's relatives went back to the village and found the woman. She said, "There was a group of Armenians that came by here, and one of the women had a baby and left it under a tree, wrapped in her clothing." The Kurdish woman showed her what the baby had been wrapped in, and gave her back the little girl. It took a long long time for my cousin to believe the child was really her baby.

After a few months' walking, we met some Kurds who said they would take us to safety. They demanded that we give them all the rest of our money and valuables first, which we did. A Turkish officer rode up with his soldiers and told us what the Kurds were really planning to do to us, that he had just learned that they had killed other refugees after telling them the same story; and then he took them to the nearby city of Urfa and had them all put to death for their crimes. When he returned to where we were camped, he gave us back everything those Kurds had stolen from us. He was a very nice man, but because everybody was stealing from us, we thought he must be a thief, too. We told him that we had money in the bank at home and when we got back there we would send it to him if only he would protect us now. He told us he felt bad about how we were being mistreated and refused to accept anything from us. He gave us permission to stay in some stables nearby, the seven or eight families that still survived. With some of the money we had left we bought bread and whatever else was

available that we could afford. All the families together would buy a cow and cook the meat and share it. We lived like that in those stables for two or three months.

Besides being cold in the wintertime, we were scared all the time about what was going to happen to us. Anything was possible. Once I was alone on a nearby hillside and a Turk came up to me and said, "Come on, I'm going to take you away with me. I will marry you, and you will have a very nice life." I said, "Go away!" But not nicely like that. I used very bad language. He thought I must be a boy to use dirty words, so he left me alone. Many times my people would dress girls in boys' clothing so the Turks wouldn't take them away to be killed.

When I got back to the stables and told my aunt what had happened, she decided to put boys' clothes on me to make the Turks think I really was a boy and not try to take me away again. It didn't feel strange to be wearing them, because when I was a little girl I used to want to be a boy.

There were a couple of soldiers who wanted to marry two women who were with us, and of course they didn't want to get married to Turks, who could have more than one wife if they wanted to. My sister wrote the nice Turkish officer a letter in French, and sent it with soldiers who couldn't understand that language. He wrote back, telling us all to come to Urfa and he would protect us. Meanwhile, however, the soldiers had threatened the two women that if they didn't marry them right away, they would get the Kurds to kill them. So the women were forced to do it. We felt sad when they went away.

Twelve of us went to live at the house of the officer from Urfa. It was divided with the men on one side and the women on the other, so that the men would not see the women, who had to keep their faces veiled from men's eyes. I was a young girl and could go to where the men were, but my sister and aunt and the other ladies were not allowed to.

A Turkish man who lived next door decided he was in love with my sister and wanted to marry her. She refused him, of course. The officer's mother-in-law who had been kind to us changed then and told my sister she had to marry the Turk. When she refused, she started beating her. My sister said, "You can beat me and kill me, I'm not going to marry him."

The mother-in-law then called some soldiers and told them, "You take this girl and do whatever you want to her, and then leave her to die in the mountains." One of them wanted to marry her because my sister was a very beautiful girl. She was afraid that if she didn't, he would take her away and rape her instead, so she married him.

He turned out to be a kind man, though, and I went to live with him and my sister. My brothers came to live with us, too, until the Armistice.

After the Armistice, the Armenian women who had been married to Turks against their will were let free. My sister had no intention of staying with her husband, and so she tricked him. We got away and never saw him again.

I never went back to Erzerum. I never could have borne going back. Never. I wanted to remember how it was before our lives changed, when everything was beautiful. All the holidays together, with all our family, the weddings that lasted two or three days, the christenings and name days. So many friends and relatives.

I feel very bitter about what the Turks did to us. If I was able, I would shoot them all to death. How can they now deny what they did? There are so many people who are now living and saw it. We are old, but there are still some of us who remain, and we remember.

BIBLIOGRAPHY

Anderson, Karen. *Wartime Women: Sex Roles, Family Relations, and the Status of Women During World War II.* Westport, Conn.: Greenwood Press, 1981.

Arendt, Hannah. *Men in Dark Times.* New York: Harcourt, Brace and World, 1955.

Berkin, Carol and Clara Lovett, eds. *Women, War and Revolution.* New York: Holmes & Meier, 1980.

Byrd, Barthy. *Homefront: Women and Vietnam.* Berkeley: Shameless Hussy Press, 1986.

Cambridge Women's Peace Collective. *My Country is the Whole World: An anthology of Women's Work of Peace and War.* Boston: Pandora, 1984.

Chodorow, Nancy. *The Reproduction of Mothering: Psychoanalysis and the Sociology of Gender.* Berkeley: Univ. of California Press, 1978.

Enloe, Cynthia. *Does Khaki Become You? The Militarization of Women's Lives.* Boston: South End Press, 1983.

Frank, Miriam, Marilyn Ziebarth and Connie Field. *The Life and Times of Rosie the Riveter.* Emeryville, Calif.: Clarity Educational Projects, 1982.

Friedlander, Judith, et al., eds. *Women in Culture and Politics: A Century of Change.* Bloomington: Indiana Univ. Press, 1986.

Goldman, Nancy Loring, ed. *Female Soldiers, Combatants or Noncombatants: Historical and Contemporary Perspectives.* Westport, Conn.: Greenwood Press, 1982.

Hartmann, Susan M. *The Home Front and Beyond: American Women in the 1940's.* Boston: Twayne, 1982.

Honey, Maureen. *Creating Rosie the Riveter: Class, Gender and Propaganda During World War II.* Amherst: Univ. of Massachusetts Press, 1984.

Keil, Sally Van Wagenen. *Those Wonderful Women In Their Flying Machines*. New York: Ranson, Wade Publishers, 1979.

Laska, Vera, ed. *Women in the Resistance and the Holocaust*. Westport, Conn.: Greenwood Press, 1983.

Mansfield, Sue. *The Gestalts of War*. New York: Dial Press, 1982.

Myles, Bruce. *Night Witches: The Untold Story of Soviet Women in Combat*. Novato, Calif.: Presidio Press, 1981.

Robinson, Lillian. *Sex, Class, and Culture*. Bloomington: Indiana Univ. Press, 1978.

Rogan, Helen. *Mixed Company: Women in the Modern Army*. Boston: Beacon, 1981.

Rowbatham, Sheila. *Women, Resistance and Revolution*. New York: Vintage, 1974.

Rupp, Leica. *Mobilizing Women for War*. Princeton: Princeton Univ. Press, 1978.

Thompson, Dorothy, ed. *Over Our Dead Bodies: Women Against the Bomb*. London: Virago Press, 1983.

Van Devanter, Lynda. *Home Before Midnight: The Story of an Army Nurse in Vietnam*. New York: Beaufort Books, 1983.

Valiant Women